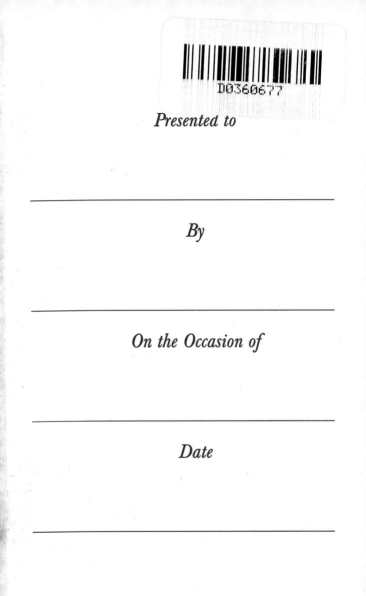

Presented to

_____

By

_____

On the Occasion of

_____

Date

_____

RUTH ANNE MUIR

Collected Thoughts on a Noble Calling

THE
HEART
OF A
TEACHER

Arielle

BARBOUR BOOKS
An Imprint of Barbour Publishing, Inc.

Scripture quotations marked NIV are taken from the HOLY BIBLE, NEW INTERNATIONAL VERSION®. NIV®. Copyright © 1973, 1978, 1984 by International Bible Society. Used by permission of Zondervan Publishing House. All rights reserved.

Scripture quotations marked NCV are taken from the New Century Version of the Bible, Copyright © 1987, 1988, 1991, Word Publishing. Used by permission.

Scripture quotations marked NKJV are taken from the New King James Version. Copyright © 1979, 1980, 1982 by Thomas Nelson, Inc. Used by permission. All rights reserved.

Scripture quotations marked NASB are taken from the New American Standard Bible, © 1960, 1962, 1963, 1968, 1971, 1972, 1973, 1975, 1977 by the Lockman Foundation. Used by permission.

Scripture quotations marked NRSV are taken from the New Revised Standard Version Bible, copyright 1989, Division of Christian Education of the National Council of the Churches of Christ in the United States of America. Used by permission. All rights reserved.

Scripture quotations marked NLT are taken from the Holy Bible, New Living Translation, copyright © 1996. Used by permission of Tyndale House Publishers, Inc. Wheaton, Illinois 60189, U.S.A. All rights reserved.

Produced with the assistance of The Livingstone Corporation. Project staff includes Ruth Anne Muir, Paige Drygas, and Christopher D. Hudson.

Published by Barbour Books, an imprint of Barbour Publishing, Inc., P.O. Box 719, Uhrichsville, Ohio 44683, www.barbourbooks.com

ECPA Member of the Evangelical Christian Publishers Association

Printed in the United States of America.

Contents

Contents

INTRODUCTION

Teaching is a priceless gift. God has given teachers special abilities to explain academic concepts, to shape students' characters, to lead them, and to encourage them to develop certain talents. The most talented teachers are not the product of strong education programs. The best teachers are those whose hearts are truly in their work.

Those who give their hearts to teaching find their hearts filled in return. The satisfaction that comes is a deep sense of worthwhile labor, of realizing just how many lives their teaching has touched. Teachers sow seeds in the fields of young minds, and their impact on students cannot be measured. Teachers shape the thoughts and character of future generations.

This book is intended to energize teachers—both those who have just begun and those who have been teaching for many years. The stories and reflections will help young teachers maintain their initial excitement, and help those teachers who are burned out to regain their first joy. For experienced teachers who continue to enjoy what they do, these stories and thoughts should encourage them to keep going, to find new ways of enjoying their students, and to gain ideas for when and how to take refreshing breaks.

Having a sense of purpose in the teaching profession can make an incredible difference in the classroom. When students know that their teachers care about them and want to teach them, they are more apt to listen and to learn. Students can sense the heart of a teacher.

Teaching involves so much more than giving students formulas to learn and facts to memorize. By seeing potential in students and encouraging their development, teachers have the opportunity to change their students' lives forever.

ABUNDANCE

I am the gate.
Whoever enters by me will be saved,
and will come in and go out and find pasture.
The thief comes only to
steal and kill and destroy.
I came that they may have life,
and have it abundantly.

JOHN 10:9–10 NRSV

GOD'S HIGHEST CALLING

Jesus promised us the abundant life—life to the fullest. The problem is, we so often search for fulfillment in other things, without realizing that it is through Christ alone that all the fullness of life is realized. We are told that the pursuit of happiness is our right, and that it can be achieved through our own efforts. So we pursue those things that we think will make us happy and act surprised when they fall short of our hopes. The family, the job, the new car, that dream vacation or dream house—some think that these things will make them happy, and to some extent they do. But these things should be the overflow of our joy, not the mainstay. If we pin all our happiness on the people and things in our lives, we will inevitably be disappointed.

The One who created us is the only One who can reach the deepest part of our spirits. It makes sense. He knows and formed our inmost parts, so He knows how best to fulfill us. Without a relationship with God, the search for meaning in life will fail. A fun, challenging job that uses our talents and skills can bring some satisfaction, but if we begin with a relationship with God, that job will bring added fulfillment to an already satisfied life. Once we have a relationship with Christ, other things in our lives will continue to contribute to our happiness, and we can sense that the Lord has given us a cornucopia—a horn of plenty, full of good things. For those who have been gifted to teach, combining a meaningful calling with a relationship with Christ is life to the fullest.

The closer we are to Christ, the more readily we see the world through His eyes. He helps us to recognize where the pieces of our lives should fit and which have priority over others. Spending time with Him changes our perspective, and then we truly can see His plan for our lives. He knows what each of us needs even better than we do. Though we don't all have the same things, we do have what is good.

PIED BEAUTY

Glory be to God for dappled things—
For skies of couple-colour as a brinded cow;
For rose-moles all in stipple upon trout that swim;
Fresh-firecoal chestnut-falls; finches' wings;
Landscape plotted and pieced—fold, fallow,
    and plough,
And all trades, their gear and tackle and trim.
All things counter, original, spare, strange;
Whatever is fickle, freckled (who knows how?)
With swift, slow; sweet, sour; adazzle, dim;
He fathers-forth whose beauty is past change:
Praise him.

GERARD MANLEY HOPKINS

Be at rest once more, O my soul,
    for the LORD has been good to you.
For you, O LORD, have delivered my soul from death,
      my eyes from tears,
      my feet from stumbling,
    that I may walk before the LORD
      in the land of the living.

PSALM 116:7–9 NIV

WHAT'S MISSING?

Since he had always known exactly what he wanted to be when he grew up, it was no surprise to anyone when Steve Cross became a teacher. He remembered that his first weeks and months had been as fun and exciting as he knew they would be (although of course he had a ton of hard work). He planned lessons, thought of creative new ways to teach, spent hours grading homework, and watched excitedly for the eyes of students to light up when they learned new concepts. Steve enjoyed teaching, and his students loved him. Within a few years, the school gave him tenure, and he settled into the security of a job he loved.

But after a few years, he couldn't understand why it was no longer enough. The excitement had slowly worn off, and although he still enjoyed teaching and the students, it didn't seem to satisfy him as it once had. Maybe this was a midlife crisis, he thought. But by this point, he did not want to change careers. He loved teaching. It was what he had always dreamed of doing. He couldn't imagine himself doing anything else.

One Saturday, Steve told his friend David about his struggle. Maybe no one is ever really happy, he reasoned. Maybe he just needed to accept that it couldn't always be that fulfilling. Maybe this was the best he could hope for in life. There was no reason why he shouldn't be happy with what he had–great job, good friends, a good balance of fun and work. What was missing? David listened patiently to Steve's thoughts and then asked him if he would come to church with him the next day. Inwardly, Steve groaned. But it was an area of his life he had ignored for a long time. He grew up in church but had moved on. He decided it couldn't hurt, so he went.

During the service, something clicked in Steve's mind. It wasn't so much the pastor's words or the friendliness of the people. When they sang, Steve felt a stirring in his heart, and he realized that what was missing in his life was God. He couldn't get that thought out of his head. Alone in his kitchen that afternoon, Steve spoke with God for the first time in a long time. He didn't know the right words to say, but he knew he had found what was missing.

The rest of the afternoon and evening he graded papers, and the week at school moved along normally. But during the week, Steve no longer felt alone. He could sense God's presence with him, and it gave him a new sense of hope. It wasn't a midlife crisis–it was a God crisis. Life took on a new vibrancy for him. With God in the center of his life, the other gifts God had given him, like his work and his friends, filled out the corners of his life. With teaching in its proper place, he no longer felt that pressure to draw every bit of meaning in his life from his job. He felt free to relax and enjoy his work for what it really was–a blessing from God, not a reason for existence.

THE PRESENCE

I sit within my room and joy to find
That Thou who always loves art with me here,
That I am never left by Thee behind,
But by Thyself Thou keep'st me ever near;
The fire turns brighter when with Thee I look,
And seems a kinder servant sent to me;
With gladder heart I read Thy holy book,
Because Thou art the eyes by which I see;
This aged chair, that table, watch, and door
Around in ready service ever wait;
Nor can I ask of Thee a menial more
To fill the measure of my large estate,
For Thou Thyself, with all a Father's care,
Where'er I turns, art ever with me there.

JONES VERY

APPRECIATION

You are the light of the world.
A city built on a hill cannot be hid.
No one after lighting a lamp
puts it under the bushel basket,
but on the lampstand,
and it gives light to all in the house.
In the same way,
let your light shine before others,
so that they may see your good works
and give glory to your Father in heaven.

MATTHEW 5:14–16 NRSV

GOD'S BEST

Everyone likes being appreciated. When we invest our time and ourselves into something, it's nice to know that our efforts are recognized. Simple words of encouragement and recognition make teaching so much more rewarding. Even though many parents and strudents may feel that sense of gratitude, few take the time to express it. Even then, God sees all our good deeds and our large and small sacrifices. Ultimately, we work for Him. He wants us to offer Him our very best. As much as we desire that affirmation from other people, we can always be assured that God knows how much we work. Whether the verbal affirmation comes or not, He will give us our true reward.

THE THANK-YOU NOTE

Peter was in the seventh grade when he discovered that he liked school. Learning had always been difficult for him, but he put extra time into his homework and earned pretty good grades. He did not think he was very smart because he couldn't think fast enough to answer his teacher's questions in class, but he kept working at it. One day, Miss Hall told him what a good student he was. He couldn't wait for school to end so he could tell his mom. After that, he worked harder than ever so that he could make Miss Hall proud of him. He spent more time doing his homework, and soon he was able to answer some of the questions in class.

A few weeks before the end of school, the class broke up into groups for a special project. Peter thought the other students wouldn't want him to be in their group, but he was wrong. They had so much fun studying the Civil War that they actually called one another outside of class to talk about it. They learned how important every person is and that nobody should be a slave. That impressed Peter. When all of the groups came back together, Peter's group wanted him to be their spokesman. What a proud day! Yes, he decided that he did like school after all.

Before school let out for the summer, Peter decided one night to write a letter to Miss Hall. He wouldn't have thought of it, but he had raved over the class so much that his mom suggested he thank his teacher.

> *Dear Miss Hall,*
> *Thank you for being my teacher and for show-*
> *ing me how much fun school can be. I had a*
> *great time in your class. Especially learning*
> *about the Civil War. What I learned most is*
> *that people are important, and no one should*
> *be a slave. I think you're important, too.*
> *Peter*

Peter went on to high school and later to college, and although he always had to work very hard to keep up, he enjoyed learning. He never forgot about Miss Hall, who encouraged him as a student and taught him just how valuable he was.

> *Education is not filling a bucket*
> *but lighting a fire.*
>
> WILLIAM BUTLER YEATS

LIFE IMPACT

A woman attended her twenty-year high school reunion. There she encountered her freshman year art teacher. She told him that she decided to go to college as a result of his inspiration, and that she was an art professor now at a large state university.

At the end of the evening's festivities, the teacher searched out his former student, shook her hand, and said, "Thank you for saying those nice things about my teaching. You've really made my day."

"You're welcome," said the woman as she hugged him, "But let me thank you–you've made my life!"

There is usually a good teacher
behind every good student.
Whether or not a student remembers
to thank his teacher,
the influence lives on in the student.

ANONYMOUS

ASPIRATION

I will make you a great nation;
I will bless you
And make your name great;
And you shall be a blessing.
I will bless those who bless you,
And I will curse him who curses you;
And in you all the families of the earth shall be blessed.

GENESIS 12:2–3 NKJV

Extraordinary Meaning

There is something deeply ingrained in the human soul that wants to achieve greatness in life. To reach beyond ourselves, to have others remember us for some great thing we have said or done or written long after we are gone is so much a part of us that it is hard to live without pursuing it in some way. But if we do not aspire to know God in an intimate way, all other pursuits will be meaningless. He needs to be our first priority, the first relationship we seek, before anything else in life. The greatest thing we can possibly aspire to is to be like Christ. The closer we are to Him, the more like Him we become. If we want recognition, that which we get from Christ is the best we can ever receive. We can aspire to be better in every area of our lives, including our professions. Naturally, we enjoy the human recognition. But we may have to redefine our terms for success as we journey through life.

Teachers can become great in the way they teach and in the way they interact with students. If they move beyond the ordinary task of teaching and reach into their students' lives, then they can achieve greatness. Though the whole world may not remember that extraordinary teacher, the student most certainly will.

Often, people desire extra recognition from others so that they will feel good about themselves, but this cheapens the meaning of doing something great. Anything truly worth doing is worthwhile in and of itself, not because of the attention that it draws to the person who does it. Greatness can be achieved through living an ordinary life in an extraordinary way. What God thinks of us is so much more important than what others think of us.

A Great Mission

Ever since she was a young girl, Margaret had wanted to be a missionary. She had heard all of the stories in church about the foreign mission field. She just knew that God wanted to use her life in a special way, and the best way she could imagine was to become a missionary. She went to college with the thought that she would remain single so she could do God's work on the mission field. Margaret didn't know what major to choose, so she sought the advice of a career counselor on campus. After testing her for interests and skills, the counselor told her that she would make an excellent teacher.

Margaret went back to her dorm room with conflicting emotions. It was fun to think about pursuing a career as a teacher, and she thought she would be good at it. But what about missions? What about the great work she wanted to do for God? Then the thought occurred to her that she could use her teaching gift overseas. Now that was exciting to think about!

Toward the end of her junior year in college, Margaret met a wonderful man, and three years later they were married. It concerned her, though, that he didn't feel called to the mission field. She struggled with that conflict for a long time but did not know how to resolve their different dreams.

So they settled into life in the States, and Margaret got a job at a local junior high school. Two years later she was tenured, and she knew only the Lord could have gotten her such a secure job so quickly. She loved her job, and she loved her students. But year after year, she wondered how she was going to achieve something great for God since she couldn't go to the mission field. She was doing the very best job she could, but it seemed so ordinary. Oh, she knew that she couldn't win God's love or His grace and mercy, but still she wanted to do something spectacular for God.

The years passed. When Margaret retired, she felt sad as she looked back over many years—all of the memories and all of the students who had come and gone. That night the administration put on a retirement dinner for her, but she was not looking forward to it. The dinner was just one more tangible reminder that she was leaving a position that she had always loved, and she did not want to be reminded of it.

During dessert, the principal got up to say a few words about Margaret and how much the staff and faculty appreciated her contributions and her deep compassion for the kids. Someone opened the door to the private room where they were having the party, and she saw a dozen faces she hadn't seen for years. One by one, they stepped to the podium and spoke about how much Margaret had changed their lives when they were in junior high school. One student had a learning disability. Because of her patience, he had gone on to get his Masters in psychology and had become a licensed counselor. Another student had grown up with a very difficult home life and had been nearly unmanageable in school. Margaret had always been firm with him, yet she also encouraged him to move past the hurt and anger to become a better person. He had become a missionary in Nigeria, and he told her that without her influence, he never would have made it. Though others had helped and encouraged him along the way, Margaret had been the first.

By this time, tears were running down her face, and her husband handed her a tissue. He had always been at her side. As one student after another shared the ways in which Margaret had influenced their lives, she realized that she had achieved greatness in the eyes of her students. And by the end of the evening, she felt the Lord telling her, "Well done," for the task He had given her. She did not need the mission field in order to achieve greatness in life. She only needed to do the very best job she could with what the Lord had given her. For the first time, she saw that her mission field was the classroom where she had spent her career.

For my thoughts are not your thoughts,
neither are your ways my ways," declares the LORD.
"As the heavens are higher than the earth,
so are my ways higher than your ways
and my thoughts than your thoughts.
As the rain and the snow
come down from heaven,
and do not return to it
without watering the earth
and making it bud and flourish,
so that it yields seed for the sower and
bread for the eater,
so is my word that goes out from my mouth:
It will not return to me empty,
but will accomplish what I desire
and achieve the purpose for which I sent it.
You will go out in joy
and be led forth in peace;
the mountains and hills
will burst into song before you,
and all the trees of the field
will clap their hands.
Instead of the thornbush will grow the pine tree,
and instead of briers the myrtle will grow.
This will be for the LORD's *renown,*
for an everlasting sign,
which will not be destroyed."

ISAIAH 55:8–13 NIV

PLAYGROUND PERSPECTIVE

A certain elementary principal was asked to pick his all-time outstanding teacher. To the surprise of many, he bypassed eminently qualified teachers, bright and shining stars in the firmament of education. His choice? A white-haired, young-at-heart grandmother who joined in playground games although nearing retirement.

When asked to explain his choice, the principal's eyes took on a faraway look. He said quietly, "Many are excellent teachers of subject material of facts and figures, but Pearl teaches students. She makes a difference in their lives."[*]

---

[*] Reece, Colleen L., and Anita Corrine Donihue. *Apples for a Teacher: A Bushel of Stories, Poems, and Prayers* (Uhrichsville, Ohio: Barbour Publishing, Inc., 1998), 17.

CALLING

*The gifts he gave were that
some would be apostles, some prophets,
some evangelists, some pastors and teachers,
to equip the saints for the work of ministry,
for building up the body of Christ,
until all of us come to the unity of the faith
and of the knowledge of the Son of God,
to maturity, to the measure
of the full stature of Christ.*

EPHESIANS 4:11–13 NRSV

A Meaningful Song

Teaching is a calling. Someone pursues teaching not to make a lot of money but to make a difference in the lives of students. Another teacher may have a passion for a certain subject or such innate talent for teaching that she cannot imagine doing anything else.

Mary Ann Musciano taught voice lessons. She met a shy, sixteen-year-old girl in church one Sunday. The girl was very quiet and somewhat depressed, but she wanted to learn to sing better. Mrs. Musciano took her on as a student.

At first, the girl was timid and sang very softly. But over time, she learned to sing well. As she gained confidence in her voice, her confidence grew in every area of her life. The girl had fun with Mrs. Musciano. She learned how to sing Italian arias, and she slowly came out of her shell.

The life of one lonely girl was changed because a voice teacher took interest in her. Truly, the most valuable lesson she learned was not about singing, but about being herself.

Having a sense of calling gives meaning to one's work. Everyone needs a job in order to pay the bills. Since our jobs take most of our waking hours, what a blessing it is to invest those hours in something meaningful. Working with a true sense of calling gives meaning to the long days, and Christ gives blessings that far exceed a paycheck.

Jesus said to them again,
"Peace be with you.
As the Father has sent me, so I send you."

JOHN 20:21 NRSV

A RARE FIND

When General Dwight Eisenhower was president, he invited writer James Michener to an occasion at the White House. Mr. Michener replied, "Dear Mr. President, I received your wonderful invitation three days after I had agreed to speak a few words at a dinner honoring the wonderful high school teacher who taught me to write. I know that you will not miss me at your dinner, but she might at hers."

With understanding, the president answered, "In a lifetime a man can live under fifteen or sixteen presidents, but a really fine teacher comes into his life but rarely."

You can be one of those rare teachers in the lives of your students. Most days you may not recognize the impact that you leave on a child's life. As you trudge through lesson plans, homework, and indifferent attitudes, you may at times feel discouraged. But the big picture is that each moment of discouragement is an opportunity to plant a lasting seed that will sprout into creativity, progress, confidence, and success. The very students who discourage you need you more than you can imagine.

I am the vine; you are the branches. If a man remains in me and I in him, he will bear much fruit; apart from me you can do nothing. If anyone does not remain in me, he is like a branch that is thrown away and withers; such branches are picked up, thrown into the fire and burned. If you remain in me and my words remain in you, ask whatever you wish, and it will be given you. This is to my Father's glory, that you bear much fruit, showing yourselves to be my disciples. . .

I no longer call you servants, because a

servant does not know his master's business.
Instead, I have called you friends, for everything
that I learned from my Father I have made
known to you. You did not choose me, but I
chose you and appointed you to go and bear
fruit—fruit that will last. Then the Father will
give you whatever you ask in my name.

JOHN 15:5–8, 15–16 NIV

TEACHING FOR LIFE

Virginia lived in the mountains in Kentucky and grew up riding her horse up and down the Appalachian Mountains as if they were her own backyard. She was a rough little mountain girl, with her braids always falling out, and she was used to some hard living. She grew up loving the Lord and hearing about Jesus in Sunday School.

When she got older, the Sunday School superintendent asked her if she would consider teaching the little children every Sunday. In her heart, Virginia knew this was what she wanted to do more than anything, and she knew Jesus wanted her to do it, too. She fumbled a little in the beginning, but soon she grew comfortable in her job and taught the children about the Lord with great joy and intensity.

Many years later, a former student came to talk to Virginia. Although she was in her eighties, she was still teaching, and Bill was concerned about her. After all, she had worked for many years and had earned the chance to retire from teaching. Bill thought she deserved some rest from the hard toil of life.

"Why should I quit?" she asked him. Her call to teach was so clear that age did not diminish it. Still, at the age of one hundred and four, she taught at three different churches every Sunday and loved it.

A PSALM OF LIFE

Tell me not, in mournful numbers,
Life is but an empty dream!
For the soul is dead that slumbers,
And things are not what they seem.

Life is real! Life is earnest!
And the grave is not its goal;
Dust thou art, to dust returnest,
Was not spoken of the soul.

Not enjoyment, and not sorrow,
Is our destined end or way;

But to act, that each tomorrow
Finds us farther than today.

Lives of great men all remind us
We can make our lives sublime,
And, departing, leave behind us
Footprints on the sands of time;

Footprints, that perhaps another,
Sailing o'er life's solemn main,
A forlorn and shipwrecked brother,
Seeing, shall take heart again.

Let us, then, be up and doing,
With a heart for any fate;
Still achieving, still pursuing,
Learn to labour and to wait.

HENRY WADSWORTH LONGFELLOW

I said, "What shall I do, Lord?"
And the Lord told me, ". . .you will be told
all that you are to do."

ACTS 22:10 NLT

THE PATH OF DEVOTION

Many have asked what could be the secret of the amazing devotion and power in the life of Paul. Acts 22:10 suggests one answer.

At the time of his conversion, as soon as he knew who it was that called him, he surrendered himself to the will of the Lord. "What shall I do, Lord?"

His life was so wonderfully fruitful because he remained true to those words.

The Lord has a will for each of us, a plan by which He wants us to live. He wants to make His will known to each one. He wants us to ask Him to reveal His will.

Such a request sincerely made implies willingness to give oneself to His will and service.

We may be sure He will answer such prayer. He will lead the child who wants to be led.

ANDREW MURRAY (1828–1917) *

---

*"Walk with Andrew Murray," *Closer Walk,* February 2000 (Atlanta: Walk Thru the Bible Ministries), 30.

CHALLENGES

O Sovereign LORD!
You have made the heavens
and earth by your great power.
Nothing is too hard for you!

JEREMIAH 32:17 NLT

Looking Past the Prickles

Jewish people born in Israel are often known as "sabra," which is a cactus with a hard, prickly outer shell, but with a soft interior. This cactus grows in harsh weather in the Middle East—hot days and cool nights. The exterior flesh is hard, thick, and prickly in order to protect the soft interior. The sabra represents what many people have become. Some people have hard exteriors due to the harsh circumstances in their lives. Perhaps they are neglected, verbally abused, or even beaten. Perhaps everyone they ever trusted betrayed them in some way. If they risk trusting someone else, they risk exposing the sensitive, vulnerable parts of themselves again, and they fear that it's not safe.

But the Scripture says that nothing is too hard for God. He sees past the unattractive outer shell to the vulnerable person inside, and He knows what has shaped each child. As teachers, we may see the faces of several sabras in our classrooms every day. Only through God's wisdom can we learn to see as

He sees, to peer past the tough skin of the more challenging students who fill our classes. It requires much more time, patience, and love, but with the Lord's help, teachers may be able to bring out the tender, inner person who is hiding in fear but who wants so desperately to be known and loved.

Blessed are the merciful, for they shall receive mercy.
Blessed are the pure in heart, for they shall see God.
Blessed are the peacemakers, for they shall be called
sons of God.

Matthew 5:7–9 NASB

YOUR PATIENCE

Within seconds of entering a room, young Ellen antagonized every living creature she saw. She would grab a guinea pig and shake it until it squealed. She would disobey rules in the classroom and treat other children in a patronizing manner. Whenever Ellen entered the room, everyone became upset– animals, adults, and other children. No one wanted anything to do with her. At recess she would brag to the other children about punishments the teacher or the principal had given her.

One day Ellen and her brother were taken from their home by a social worker and put into a foster home. Their mother was too sick with her pregnancy to take care of them and needed help from the state. On one of her visits, the social worker discovered that Ellen was often beaten by her father at home. The girl's mother told her of a time when Ellen picked up everything resembling a switch or a belt and threw it out the window. But that did not stop the abuse. Ellen acted the way she did because she had to be tough to endure the treatment her father gave her.

Ellen softened a little with the love and patience her foster family gave her, but she and her brother were back home again a month later. However, the foster family clued Ellen's teacher in to what her home life was like. The teacher befriended Ellen. She was determined to see the best in the mischeivous little girl. Eventually, Ellen revealed more of her sensitive, inner self to her teacher, and her attitudes began to change. Even though her home life did not change, Ellen began to like people who were not hurting her, and they in turn began to like her.

Challenging students are hard to manage. How can you know how to respond to them? They need clear rules, but they also need love and acceptance. This is a hard balance for a teacher to achieve.

With God's help, you can discover the right way to handle each student. The wisdom comes from Him.

O Lord, you have searched me
  and you know me.
You know when I sit and when I rise;
  you perceive my thoughts from afar.
You discern my going out and my lying down;
  you are familiar with all my ways.
Before a word is on my tongue
  you know it completely, O Lord.

PSALM 139:1–4 NIV

OUTWITTED

He drew a circle that shut me out–
Heretic, rebel, a thing to flout.
But Love and I had the wit to win:
We drew a circle that took him in!

EDWIN MARKHAM

A GARDEN OF HOPE

Joel and Michelle work with students in an inner-city neighborhood. Every kid presents some new little challenges. The youth center where they meet after school for tutoring, projects, and basketball is on the border between two different gangs, and the center is considered neutral territory. They hope to prevent the elementary kids from getting involved with the gangs by giving them other options –having their own close community and helping them to discover their academic potential. Some of the high school students are only involved in the program for the use of the gym. Others really want to do well in school, and they are motivated by all the tutoring help they receive.

When Joel and Michelle first moved to the neighborhood, they decided to grow a garden in the yard of the church-owned building where they lived. First, they had to clean out the trash that had been accumulating for many years. They found twenty-year-old newspapers, broken beer bottles, and other trash that had either blown in or been dumped there. Then they tilled the soil, planned what they wanted to grow, and planted the seeds. They put up a little fence around their small garden to keep people from walking over it. They watered their garden and prayed that it would grow. After two years, Joel and Michelle noticed a little bit of fragile grass poking through the soil. The ground had not produced anything for many years, so they knew this was progress.

They often use the analogy of their garden to describe their work with the students. Trash has either blown into their young lives or been dumped there, and it takes a long time to clear the trash out. Some of the trash will always be there—emotional scars that can heal but can never be removed. The soil of their lives has not been prepared for planting anything that will grow, and it needs patient work. The seeds that are planted often do not grow, but sometimes a little bit of green pokes up. The first signs of growth in the students must be carefully protected.

When Joel and Michelle plant love and trust into these kids, they eventually see responses, and the changes can be dramatic. A formerly sulky and angry student learns to smile and laugh with delight. A failing student lights up when he brings them a report card with a good grade. A neglected child finds someone who wants to spend time with him, and the impact is incredible. Though the garden is fragile, it is growing, and the gardeners are slowly seeing that their efforts and tears and prayers are actually producing growth in the lives of these tough kids.

*The good soil represents the hearts of
those who truly accept God's message
and produce a huge harvest—
thirty, sixty, or even a hundred times
as much as had been planted.*

MATTHEW 13:23 NLT

COMPASSION

The Lord is gracious and merciful,
slow to anger and abounding in steadfast love.
The Lord is good to all,
and his compassion is over all that he has made.

PSALM 145:8–9 NRSV

LISTENING TO THE HEART

When others show compassion toward us, they make us feel worthwhile and cared for. A compassionate person not only listens to our words but also hears what our hearts are saying. Students long for the same compassion. It is easier to feel compassion for the shy students who are on the outer edges of the group than it is to show that same compassion to the sulky or angry students who continually try our patience.

Too many times, we withhold our compassion because of anger or impatience. It's tough not to take out the negative feelings on the troublesome students. It may not even be the students who are irritating us. Our own feelings of being unappreciated, overlooked, or taken for granted may set us on edge. However tempting it may be, teachers must learn to not turn our frustration, impatience, and anger on those whom God has entrusted to our care.

Students respond to anger with deep hurt, whether they show it or not. We can all remember a time when someone was unreasonably angry with us—perhaps even in the last week. The effect is usually devastating. But compassion heals the hidden wounds, especially in impressionable students.

The student who is especially shy needs encouragement, and the student who is extra sulky might have a harsh home life. Compassion can help students blossom. A teenager who has never been shown compassion may become a tenderhearted boy once he receives it.

> *The LORD is merciful and gracious;*
> *he is slow to get angry*
> *and full of unfailing love.*
>
> PSALM 103:8 NLT

LOVE'S LIFELINE

Years ago a Johns Hopkins' professor gave a group of graduate students this assignment: Go to the slums. Take two hundred boys, between the ages of twelve and sixteen, and investigate their background and environment. Then predict their chances for the future.

THE HEART OF A TEACHER

After consulting social statistics, talking to the boys, and compiling much data, the students concluded that 90 percent of the boys would spend some time in jail.

Twenty-five years later, another group of graduate students was given the job of testing the prediction. They went back to the same area. Some of the boys—by then men—were still there, a few had died, and some had moved away. They were able to contact one hundred eighty of the original two hundred. They found that only four of the group had ever been sent to jail.

Why was it that these men, who had lived in a breeding place of crime, had such a surprisingly good record? The researchers were continually told, "Well, there was a teacher. . ."

They pressed further, and found that in 75 percent of the cases, it was the same woman. The researchers went to this teacher, now living in a retirement home. How had she exerted this remarkable influence over that group of children? Could she give them any reason why these boys should have remembered her?

"No," she said. "No, I really couldn't." And then, thinking back over the years, she said musingly, more to herself than to her questioners, "I loved those boys. . . ."

Yet the LORD longs to be gracious to you;
  he rises to show you compassion.
For the LORD is a God of justice.
  Blessed are all who wait for him!

ISAIAH 30:18 NIV

KIND WORD, OPEN HEART

"Those who minister the Gospel should be gentle, tender, and affectionate.

"Nothing is ever gained by a sour, harsh, crabby, dissatisfied manner. Sinners are never scolded into either duty or heaven. No man is a better or more faithful preacher because he is rough in manner, coarse or harsh in his expressions, or sour in his speech. Not thus was either the Master or Paul.

"There is no crime in being polite and courteous; and there is no piety in outraging all the laws which promote happy communication.

"What is wrong we should indeed oppose—but it should be in the kindest manner towards those who do wrong. What is true and right we should maintain and defend—and we shall always do it more effectively if we do it kindly."

ALBERT BARNES (1798–1870)*

---

*"Walk with Albert Barnes," *Closer Walk,* June 2000 (Atlanta: Walk Thru the Bible Ministries), 9.

THE ART OF ENCOURAGEMENT

Laura Loveberry was a traveling art teacher, and in the course of a two-week period, she taught over two thousand students. Though it seemed impossible to learn every child's name, she tried her best. Laura knew that very often the new students had trouble fitting in, and some "veteran" students picked on the new ones. So at the beginning of a class, Laura excitedly asked who the new students were, so that she could give them special recognition and attention. Through experience she knew that a teacher influences the attitudes of the students toward their classmates, and she wanted the class to accept and like the new students.

During one class, Laura noticed a girl who kept her head and her gaze down at the ground, and she chewed her hair. The other students unmercifully teased her, and Laura could tell that it hurt the girl deeply. She quietly said, "Nancy, I need to talk with you." They went out into the hall together. With compassion, Laura looked at the girl and spoke reassuring words. She told the girl to ignore the teasing and the mean comments. "No matter how much it hurts, don't let it show on the outside. And one more thing—you have to stop chewing on your hair." Nancy looked up at her art teacher and nodded with some hesitation.

When Laura returned two weeks later, she had seen so many students that she had nearly forgotten the talk with Nancy. But as soon as she saw the girl, she noticed a change. Nancy's eyes were bright, her head held high, and she no longer chewed on her hair. She whispered to Laura, "Our plan is working." That's all she said. But Laura knew that the girl's life had changed and that the other students were beginning to like her. Nancy's experience reinforced Laura's belief that teachers can do much more in the lives of their students than simply execute a lesson plan. It takes compassion to see the isolated students who are hurting, and by acting on that compassion, teachers can encourage students to change their attitudes.

SPEAK GENTLY

Speak gently! It is better far
To rule by love, than fear;
Speak gently; let not harsh words mar
The good we might do here!

Speak gently! Love doth whisper low
The vows that true hearts bind;
And gently Friendship's accents flow;
Affection's voice is kind.

Speak gently to the little child!
Its love be sure to gain;
Teach it in accents soft and mild:
It may not long remain.

Speak gently to the young, for they
Will have enough to bear
Pass through this life as best they may,
'Tis full of anxious care!

Speak gently to the aged one,
Grieve not the careworn heart;
The sands of life are nearly run,
Let such in peace depart!

Speak gently, kindly, to the poor;
Let no harsh tone be heard;
They have enough they must endure,
Without an unkind word!

Speak gently to the erring–know,
They may have toiled in vain;
Perchance unkindness made them so;
Oh, win them back again!

Speak gently! He who gave His life
To bend man's stubborn will,
When elements were in fierce strife,
Said to them, "Peace, be still."

Speak gently! 'tis a little thing
Dropped in the heart's deep well;
The good, the joy, which it may bring,
Eternity shall tell.

DAVID BATES

CONFIDENCE

Have I not commanded you?
Be strong and courageous.
Do not be terrified;
do not be discouraged,
for the LORD your God will be
with you wherever you go.

JOSHUA 1:9 NIV

Courage to Overcome

As teachers, when we lack confidence in ourselves, we can quickly lose an entire day of good teaching. Fear can cause us to muddle through an hour of classwork rather than make a lasting impression. When we lack confidence, for whatever reason, our words lack authority. What may have been a passionate message dwindles into a boring lecture, and we may even appear as though we don't know our material. This kind of situation will inevitably come up in every teacher's career at some point or another. It not only affects how we feel about ourselves, but it also affects how our students perceive us. It might even determine whether or not they listen to and believe what we are saying.

Even though we may experience moments like this, we can learn to overcome them. The Lord provides the courage to say and do what we need to boldly and confidently. He gives us His strength, which is infinitely greater than ours, to see us through those tough times in life when we lack the confidence to do a certain task, for whatever reason. When we are on God's side, we become more than conquerors in Christ.

*So he said to me,
"This is the word of the LORD to Zerubbabel:
'Not by might nor by power,
but by my Spirit,' says the LORD Almighty."*

ZECHARIAH 4:6 NIV

DEPENDING ON GOD'S STRENGTH

Dan felt terrified. This was his very first year, his first day, his first class. All of the classes he had taken, all of the lessons he had planned had not prepared him for this. Why did he feel so afraid? He only wanted to go back home before he became ill. With a sickening realization, he knew that he had to go through with the day, no matter how badly he did. This was worse than taking a final without studying.

At 7:30 A.M., the students began coming in. He smiled at each one, but they barely glanced in his direction. He sweated and fumbled and plowed his way through the lesson. An hour later they were gone, and he braced himself for the next bunch of students. The day was a disaster. Dan couldn't face anyone at the end of it and quickly walked to his car rather than stopping to chat in the teacher's lounge.

Teaching. It was what he had always wanted to do. What went wrong? Why was he so afraid? His small-group leader from church called that evening to find out how it had gone. Dan tried to cover it up. He said he was fine and the day went fine, but somewhere in those words his voice trailed off into silence. Eric caught on quickly and knew that Dan was afraid. Eric reassured him that Jesus would help him overcome his fear and become a good teacher. Dan wanted that more than anything. That night he acknowledged that he could not do it on his own and that he needed help. In his faith, he came to a place of total dependence.

Dan woke up the next morning with exhilaration rather than terror. He knew he still had a lot to learn about teaching, but the fear was gone. Sure, he knew so little compared to more experienced teachers, but he was willing to learn. By relying on God's strength –instead of his own– he gained real confidence that he could do anything, even face a tough class of new students. Rather than focusing on his own weaknesses, he concentrated on God's strength.

And David said to his son Solomon, "Be strong and of good courage, and do it; do not fear nor be dismayed, for the LORD God—my God—will be with you. He will not leave you nor forsake you, until you have finished all the work for the service of the house of the LORD."

1 CHRONICLES 28:20 NKJV

It is the Lord who goes before you.
He will be with you;
he will not fail you or forsake you.
Do not fear or be dismayed.

DEUTERONOMY 31:8 NRSV

PRAYING IT OUT

For the first three years of her career, Jill Whitney absolutely hated teaching. She wondered why she had ever gotten into this profession and prayed that God would deliver her from it so she could go on to something else. She hated all of the hours outside of the classroom. She never had time for herself or her husband. Planning lessons and correcting papers always got in the way of the things she wanted to do. She resented having such a tight schedule in her life and having to attend so many meetings at school. All of the first-year teachers had to take education classes to improve their skills in specific subjects and to figure out the students' learning styles. The work never ended.

Finally, after her third year in the classroom, it started coming together. Talking with other teachers, visiting other schools, observing different teaching styles, and taking methods classes all helped to build Jill's confidence. At last, she found what she had been lacking. Her confidence brought an enjoyment of teaching. Rather than fighting against God or crying out for Him to deliver her from her career, she began to thank Him for helping her to wait it out.

LIGHT SHINING
OUT OF DARKNESS

God moves in a mysterious way,
His wonders to perform;
He plants His footsteps in the sea,
And rides upon the storm.

Deep in unfathomable mines
Of never-failing skill,
He treasures up His bright designs,
And works His sovereign will.

Ye fearful saints, fresh courage take,
The clouds ye so much dread
Are big with mercy, and shall break
In blessings on your head.

Judge not the Lord by feeble sense,
But trust Him for His grace;
Behind a frowning providence,
He hides a smiling face.

His purposes will ripen fast,
Unfolding every hour;
The bud may have a bitter taste,
But sweet will be the flower.

Blind unbelief is sure to err,
And scan His work in vain;
God is His own interpreter,
And He will make it plain.

WILLIAM COWPER
From *Olney Hymns*

DETERMINATION

Not that I have already obtained this
or have already reached the goal;
but I press on to make it my own,
because Christ Jesus has made me his own.
Beloved, I do not consider that
I have made it my own;
but this one thing I do:
forgetting what lies behind and
straining forward to what lies ahead,
I press on toward the goal for the prize of
the heavenly call of God in Christ Jesus.

PHILIPPIANS 3:12–14 NRSV

Pursuing God

Determination in our own strength will not get us far. How long did our New Year's resolutions last this year? The resolve to have a daily quiet time, to lose weight, to get in shape, to keep up with the correspondence with family and friends? How long before that new determination to really do these things wore off? How long can our personal resolve last?

When we try to meet our goals in our own strength, we are doomed to fail. Only by relying on the Spirit and asking Him for strength can we really begin to see success and growth in our lives. With Him all things are possible, and if our determination to do or to be something in life originates with Him, He will see us through it.

With determination, we can set our eyes on a concrete goal and do everything in our power to achieve it. Whatever our goals may be–to become more confident teachers, to reach certain students who are angry and sullen, to prepare lesson plans more thoroughly, to get an advanced degree, to become more gracious in our praise—we can focus on them and work wholeheartedly to achieve them. When our relationship with the Lord is strong, He gives us the strength and determination to push ahead past adversity or discouragement. But God has to be our source of strength before our determination will be effective.

*He replied,
"What is impossible from a human perspective
is possible with God."*

LUKE 18:27 NLT

WHEN GOD BREAKS THROUGH

The girl was wild and uncontrollable. She never sat down at the table to eat but ran around, unkempt, and grabbed food off the table whenever she felt hungry. Her parents were at a loss about how to help her. They finally found a woman who said she would try to help.

Anne was a young teacher with a big task. Somehow, she had to reach through the outer deterrents to the girl who could not see, hear, or speak. Somewhere there was a girl inside that needed her, and Anne was determined to reach her. Anne spent time with the girl, washing and brushing her hair and teaching her simple hygiene.

The girl did not know who this person was who treated her so gently, but she liked the attention. Her frustration grew as she was still unable to communicate with this new person in her life. Anne was patient, however, and became more determined than ever to reach the girl. She altered a form of sign language and spelled words out into the palm of the girl's hand. Anne took a book, placed it in the girl's hand, then spelled out "book" with the special sign language. Soon the girl began recognizing objects, and she was able to spell them out. She even learned how to ask for food when she was hungry. She learned how to sit down at the table and eat with her family. Anne had broken through, expanded little Helen Keller's world, and taught her how to communicate.

Before Anne came into her life, Helen had many thoughts but no way to express them. With the gift of language, she could not only ask for food when she was hungry, but she could also tell her parents how she felt. She could tell them when she was sad and when she was happy and what made her feel those emotions. Her life was dramatically changed because of the dedication of one resolute young teacher who refused to give up.

The marvelous richness of human experience would lose something of rewarding joy if there were no limitations to overcome. The hilltop hour would not be half so wonderful if there were no dark valleys to traverse.

HELEN KELLER

Work hard and cheerfully at whatever you do,
as though you were working for the Lord
rather than for people.
Remember that the Lord will give you
an inheritance as your reward,
and the Master you are serving is Christ.

COLOSSIANS 3:23–24 NLT

TEACHERS

Teachers are full of patience.
Teachers never give up.
And won't let you give up either.
Teachers take students seriously.
Teachers care in their sleep.
Teachers see the genius
In every drawing, poem, and essay.
Teachers make you feel important.
Teachers also help others.
Teachers never grow old.
Teachers stay famous in their students' minds,
Forever.

AUTHOR UNKNOWN

TEACHING THIS LOVE

Tony Robinson faced a tough assignment, teaching at a high school on New York's Lower East Side. He had been out of the teaching profession for a few years, and it was hard to start over again as the new teacher. A lot of time had passed since he'd had his last class.

He walked into his classroom on the first day, and the students ignored him. They continued talking loudly and joking around, even when he tried to get their attention. Tony knew that to get respect, you have to give respect first. He finally yelled loudly enough to be heard, and the group quit talking. Now they directed disparaging comments toward him. He looked one young lady in the eye, and checking his list, asked for her name. "Liz," she said. "Liz Johnson."

"Miss Johnson," he said, "what do you like to do in your spare time?"

The boys laughed, and Liz flirted with Tony for an answer. "Respect yourself," Tony told her and the rest of the class, "and others will also respect you."

Tony insisted on being called Mr. Robinson, and he likewise insisted on using titles and surnames as he addressed each of his high school students. They were not interested in learning from some old moldy book, so he invented new ways of gaining their interest in the world about them, in what they would do for work, in what their home lives were like and what they wanted their own homes to be like when they graduated. He earnestly sought to teach them the lessons they needed to know before they left the safe haven of high school. He knew that their lives outside of school were not ideal. Mr. Robinson also knew that the full weight of adulthood was not yet on them, and he was determined to give them the tools they would need to do well for themselves and their families. They learned respect—for themselves and for those they came into contact with. They also learned love. They knew their stern old teacher with his odd ways loved them, and before the year was out, they loved him back.

Tony knew that he could never have made progress with these hardened kids without the Lord's leading. At times, their disrespect caused him pain that he hid, and he would have given up had it not been for the example of his Lord. Jesus loves those who are so hard to love. Again and again, when he felt like giving up, he went to God for solace and for the courage and determination to persevere. And he was never disappointed.

YOU ARE MY STRENGTH

Allow yourself to fail, to forgive failure, and to learn from failures. You won't be right all of the time, you know, but God can use you, even in your weakness to serve His purposes. Whether you are a new teacher or not, your starting point must be the realization that you are the instrument and God is the strength of your teaching. Ask Him, therefore, to renew you daily–even hourly–that you may serve Him well. Your commitment to be God's tool will change your focus from performance to praise.

LORNA VAN GILST *

*Van Gilst, Lorna. *Christian Educators Journal,* October/November 1989.

ENCOURAGEMENT

*Think of ways to encourage one another
to outbursts of love and good deeds.*

HEBREWS 10:24 NLT

FRIENDLY SUPPORT

Everyone needs friends, and teachers are no exception. We are relational creatures. Friends share our disappointments and joys and give life greater meaning. Friends listen to us when we're discouraged or frustrated. Friends rejoice with us over our achievements. They help us to have fun when we've forgotten how. Friends lean on each other and hold each other up.

Some days, teachers feel discouraged about certain students or even other teachers, and it seems like no one else quite understands. Sharing with another teacher can either compound the problem or become more of a gripe session that only leaves us more frustrated. During times like these, teachers need friends who will be there to listen and encourage. Just by having someone to listen and care, a teacher can walk away feeling encouraged and appreciated.

*The heartfelt counsel of a friend is
as sweet as perfume and incense.*

PROVERBS 27:9 NLT

INFLUENTIAL WORDS

Janine had been feeling low for several months,
and she didn't know why. Her days dragged by in
the endless routine of teaching students who would
rather be somewhere else, and her evenings were
an awful continuation of correcting homework.

One night Janine tossed restlessly in bed, thinking over her predicament. She didn't have even
one friend (at least none that she could remember).
She couldn't recall the last time she had called a
friend to chat, and telemarketers were the only
ones who ever called her. Janine got out of bed,
sat down at her desk, and pulled out a piece of
paper. She wrote down every person she could
think of who had ever been a friend to her. Some
of them were scattered across the country, but
some lived nearby. Janine decided to call one
friend with whom she could start over.

Next, she listed all of the activities she did in
order to relax—at the top of the list were watching

movies and reading books. Although these things helped to relieve her stress somewhat, she knew they also isolated her from people. Janine decided she could afford the time to have a cup of coffee with a friend once a week. At least it was a start. That night she slept better than she had in a long time.

Several weeks later, Janine found herself in the middle of an uncomfortable situation with a parent. The parent accused her of being unfair in the classroom by giving more attention to the bright children than to those, like his daughter, who were slower. Janine thought she treated all of her students the same, and the confrontation made her defensive.

Later that evening, she was able to talk it over with her friend Debbie, with whom she had recently renewed a friendship. Debbie listened patiently and then talked through it with her. She encouraged her to keep an open mind and to begin noticing if and when she gave preferential treatment to some of the students.

Janine deliberately began to put more effort into reaching out to those students who were slower, and she was rewarded when the performance level of those students improved. Even though the critical parent never acknowledged his daughter's improvement, Janine received encouragement and understanding from Debbie. Having that one close friend enabled Janine to grow in new directions, confident of the support of another person.

Those are red-letter days in our lives when we meet people who thrill us like a fine poem, people whose handshake is brimful of unspoken sympathy and whose sweet, rich natures impart to our eager, impatient spirits a wonderful restlessness which, in its essence, is divine.

The perplexities, irritations, and worries that have absorbed us pass like unpleasant dreams, and we wake to see with new eyes and hear with new ears the beauty and harmony of God's real world. The solemn nothings that fill our everyday life blossom suddenly into bright possibilities.

HELEN KELLER

Some friends may ruin you, but a real friend will be more loyal than a brother.

PROVERBS 18:24 NCV

An Encouraging Gift

If you respond best to verbal affirmation, then you know what a gift your words can be. Think about your friends and who really needs extra encouragement today. Writing a short note or Bible verse can show someone just how much you care. Look for the good qualities that you see in your friends, and mention how much you admire those traits. You might be surprised at how much your friends respond to your words. What you say once in passing may remain in their minds for a lifetime.

GIVING

I have received full payment and even more;
I am amply supplied,
now that I have received
from Epaphroditus the gifts you sent.
They are a fragrant offering,
an acceptable sacrifice, pleasing to God.
And my God will meet all your needs
according to his glorious riches in Christ Jesus.

PHILIPPIANS 4:18–19 NIV

HE FILLS YOUR CUP

Teachers give so much of themselves. Teachers know the meaning of sacrifice in a very personal way. Every day and evening is devoted to their work, and they may find very little personal time. Unlike most jobs that are limited strictly to office hours, teaching requires much outside preparation. Many teachers make a lot of sacrifices to commit to their careers. Teachers sacrifice personal time, better salaries, and corporate glory. At times, teachers may feel the weight of the sacrifice, and it is helpful to step back and get a fuller perspective.

Jesus demonstrated the highest level of giving. He delighted in serving His disciples. When He took off His outer robe and knelt before them with a basin of water to wash their feet, He showed joyful, willing sacrifice. When we begin to see situations through His eyes, we will not resent having to give so much. He will teach us what it means to truly have servants' heart.

The Lord promised that He would meet our

needs–emotional, physical, and spiritual. Teaching requires giving of oneself, but it does not have to feel like a sacrifice. Jesus Himself was a teacher when He lived on earth, and His time and attention were constantly in demand. He gave His time freely, even when He was exhausted. When we feel empty, we need to let the Lord fill us so that we can in turn give to our students. When our own cups are over-flowing, we can spill over into their lives.

Dear brothers and sisters, whenever trouble comes your way, let it be an opportunity for joy. For when your faith is tested, your endurance has a chance to grow. So let it grow, for when your endurance is fully developed, you will be strong in character and ready for anything.

JAMES 1:2–4 NLT

It doesn't matter how great the pressure is. What really matters is where the pressure lies, whether it comes between me and God or whether it presses me nearer His heart.

HUDSON TAYLOR

THE ROAD OF SACRIFICE

He had never intended to teach middle school, and some days David hated his job. When his classroom was filled with overly excited kids who were constantly testing authority, he wondered if he could stand it another day.

On the way home from one particularly trying day at school, his car started bumping along the road. He pulled over to take a look at it, and he had a flat tire. *Oh, great,* he thought to himself. *The perfect ending to the perfect day.* It was cold out, and as he got down on the ground with the jack, it began to snow.

He complained bitterly to the Lord. Wasn't it enough that he got paid so little, that he was surrounded by hyper kids, that he saw so few results for all his work, and now he had a flat tire to top it all off! As he struggled to loosen the bolts, his hand slipped and smashed across a piece of metal. He saw a little cut on one of his knuckles, and it began to bleed.

David sat in the road next to his car, and as he watched his slightly bloody hand, the falling snow thickened. He put pressure on the cut and sat quietly until the blood stopped. For once, he was forced to be still. As his palm filled with blood, he was reminded of the sacrifice of his Savior.

He began reflecting on the work that God had given him to do. So often he felt unequal to his task. It occurred to him that perhaps that was what God intended. Perhaps if he always felt like he could do things on his own, then he would not recognize his constand need for Jesus' help. Instead he felt a continual sense of dependence.

His middle school class was really not that bad. When he got worn down, he had a hard time seeing the best in them. The kids just didn't know how to use their energy or how to phrase their questions about life. Everything was awkward to them at this age. But he must have been the same way at that age.

His bleeding had stopped, and he went back to changing the tire. The lesson of the moment had not been lost on him.

For it is God who works in you to will and to act according to his good purpose.

Do everything without complaining or arguing, so that you may become blameless and pure, children of God without fault in a crooked and depraved generation, in which you shine like stars in the universe.

PHILIPPIANS 2:13–15 NIV

GROWTH

*You need to persevere so that
when you have done the will of God,
you will receive what he has promised.*

HEBREWS 10:36 NIV

Fruit of Change

The only evidence of life is growth, and the only evidence of growth is change. Being a teacher provides myriad opportunities to grow personally. Every student is different and presents a whole new set of challenges and rewards.

As teachers, we can be stretched in every way—spiritual, intellectual, emotional, and relational. Being surrounded by students who are always growing and learning reminds teachers to be lifelong students themselves. Every day presents new lessons from unexpected sources, and the learning never ends.

Growth is always good, even though the process may be difficult. The apple tree that has never been pruned may have very large limbs, but the fruit will not be as big or as good. Sometimes it bears no fruit at all. The same can be true in the lives of teachers. No teacher can become satisfied with what she knows. She cannot feel overly confident that she knows everything. The smallest child can bring surprising humility to even the most experienced teacher.

Show me Your ways, O Lord;
Teach me Your paths.
Lead me in Your truth and teach me,
For You are the God of my salvation;
On You I wait all the day.

PSALM 25:4–5 NKJV

A FRESH START

After teaching for twenty years, Kathy knew she had slipped into a complacent rut. When she first graduated from college, she got a job as a teacher's aide for a couple of years while she waited for a full-time teaching position to open. When she finally found one, she was so eager to start teaching.

The years slipped by, and twenty years passed seemingly without her knowledge and certainly without her permission. She had always planned to go back to school for her master's degree but had never felt like giving up a good job at a good school.

Now she knew she had to take a chance and do it. The thought of going back to school thrilled her, and she made the decision. She and her husband had prayed about it for two years, and nothing seemed to be standing in her way. Their children were now in their teens, and they were often at school with their sports and music activities in the afternoons. Kathy would still be home in the evenings. The kids relished the thought of their mom doing homework.

It was now spring, and Kathy was running out of time to apply to different schools. She spent a weekend doing some research and then filling out necessary forms for local schools. Money would be tight, but they could make it on one income. Her school had offered to pay for half of her education, and that helped a lot. The waiting game was the worst. Kathy tried to put it to the back of her mind as she concentrated on the rest of the school year. She didn't want to cheat the students at all just because her life was about to take a sharp turn in the road.

The school of her choice finally sent her an acceptance letter, and Kathy danced a little jig of joy in the living room. Kathy had an energy and excitement for life that had been missing for awhile. This was a goal that she hadn't achieved yet, and she was incredibly eager. She wanted to learn more, she wanted to be in deep discussions about important issues with peers, she wanted that degree, and she wanted it with highest honors.

There was so much to think about. She bought a backpack on wheels so she could drag her books around without straining her back. She packed away her teaching clothes to make room for extra jeans and sweaters. That summer, Kathy really enjoyed herself and her family. She knew there would be hard times ahead, but she would make it.

The first day of class was so exciting. But she couldn't believe how young the other grad students were. It was so strange to be sitting at a desk rather than standing up front teaching. She was ready, though, and she dove into the course work with all of her newfound energy. It was harder than she thought it would be, but she got encouragement from her husband and children every day.

One day toward the end of the first term, Kathy was particularly discouraged with the volume of work she had yet to do before finals. Over dinner, Ken asked her how the day had gone, and she burst into tears. "How did I possibly think I could do this? It's too hard; the papers are too long; there isn't enough time!" She was at the end of her rope that day. Her family talked her into giving it a rest that evening, and against her better judgment, they had a family game night. She laughed along with the others but only through feelings of guilt for not working on her projects and papers.

The next day, though, she felt much better, and forged ahead on her projects. The term ended, and Kathy earned excellent marks. Over the next two years, she had to relearn how to study, how to set different priorities, how to set aside the non-essentials. She drew closer to her husband and children because she no longer had some of the clutter that had occupied her time before.

When Kathy finished school, she returned to teaching with a new zeal. She understood her high school students better since she had so recently been in school herself. From a student's perspective rather than from a teacher's, she was able to teach them about good study habits. She didn't return to her extra activities that had tied up her time before she'd returned to school. Instead, she made more time for her family.

Kathy had a fresh start on her career. She had a renewed desire to learn and grow. She could learn from her students, and she did. They, in turn, learned from her. When she acknowledged that she didn't know the answer to a question, it became a game to see who could research the answer fastest. Kathy kept her eyes open to find new things she could learn each day.

*Anyone who stops learning is old, whether at twenty
or eighty.*
Anyone who keeps learning stays young.
The greatest thing in life is to keep your mind young.
HENRY FORD

To identify teaching as an art should not
lead one to conclude that formal preparation is not required. The aptitudes that
lead to success in the classroom will not
spring to full fruition of their own accord.
Neither will the talents of painter or poet.
Only after repeated exposure to the
demands of the art and systematic development of the latent but recognizable
qualifying abilities will that person be
ready to engage in the art to which he has
been called. Jesus Himself, called Teacher
by His disciples, spent thirty years in
preparation for His brief earthly ministry.
NORMAL DE JONG,
Education in the Truth

GUIDANCE

*Your word is a lamp to my feet
and a light to my path.*

PSALM 119:105 NIV

FAITHFUL GUIDE

When God's chosen people traveled in the desert for forty years, they did not wander aimlessly. Rather, they followed wherever God led them. He guided them with a pillar of cloud by day and a pillar of fire by night. They did not know where they were going or when they would arrive, but they followed God. He led them on a long and circuitous route, but they followed His plan, knowing that they could never survive on their own.

We do not always understand why the Lord leads us along the circuitous route. Learning the lessons that He teaches us along the way is often as important as reaching the destination. Often the road seems hard, but the Lord provides enough strength for the journey. He is the One who guides, and He is the One who makes the burden of the journey lighter, if we let Him.

Along the way, the Lord puts others in our paths whom we can guide in some way. For teachers, this is a basic part of the profession. Teachers guide students every day. Teachers encourage students to pursue certain talents. Teachers help shape their students' characters. As we receive guidance from the Lord, we can in turn impart the wisdom He gives us to our students.

Happy are those whose way is blameless,
*   who walk in the law of the LORD.*
Happy are those who keep his decrees,
*   who seek him with their whole heart,*
who also do no wrong,
*   but walk in his ways.*

PSALM 119:1–3 NRSV

It's not so much
what is poured into the student,
but what is planted, that really counts.

ANONYMOUS

BELIEF IN POSSIBILITIES

Have you ever dreaded having a certain student in your class because of negative advance publicity?

You might have felt you were beaten before you got started.

Edgar A. Guest in his poem, "It Couldn't Be Done" tells of a man who wouldn't buy into this philosophy.

A certain junior high creative writing teacher also swam against the tide. She saw talent in a boy who loved to pretend all through his younger years. He hated structured tasks, seemed disorganized, and showed little promise. The teacher turned the boy loose to write, and write, and write. He went on to college and wrote some more.

One day his former teacher received a short note. "You are invited to the opening night of my first play. Complimentary tickets await you at the door. Perhaps you'll bring a student who loves to write as much as I do. Thank you for believing in me when no one else—including myself—did.""

Reece, Colleen L., and Anita Corrine Donihue. *Apples for a Teacher: A Bushel of Stories, Poems, and Prayers* (Uhrichsville, Ohio: Barbour Publishing, Inc., 1998), 21.

The Windows

Lord, how can man preach Thy eternal word?
He is a brittle, crazy glass,
Yet in Thy temple Thou dost him afford
This glorious and transcendent place,
To be a window through Thy grace.

But when Thou dost anneal in glass Thy story,
Making Thy life to shine within
The holy preachers, then the light and glory
More revered grows, and more doth win,
Which else shows wat'rish, bleak, and thin.

Doctrine and life, colors and light, in one
When they combine and mingle, bring
A strong regard and awe; but speech alone
Doth vanish like a flaring thing,
And in the ear, not conscience, ring.

GEORGE HERBERT

HOPE

Do you not know?
Have you not heard?
The LORD is the everlasting God,
the Creator of the ends of the earth.
He will not grow tired or weary,
and his understanding no one can fathom.
He gives strength to the weary
and increases the power of the weak.
Even youths grow tired and weary,
and young men stumble and fall;
but those who hope in the LORD
will renew their strength.
They will soar on wings like eagles;
they will run and not grow weary,
they will walk and not be faint.

ISAIAH 40:28–31 NIV

FOREVER HOPEFUL

Compared to the great virtues of faith and love, we hear so little about hope. Hope might not be as mighty as faith or as noble as love, but without hope, faith and love are incomplete. Only with a sense of hope can we face the dark times in our lives, trusting that God will deliver us. Only because of hope can we walk through the lonely valleys, continually hoping that times of refreshing will come.

If only we could see the situations in our lives with God's eyes rather than our own, then we would know that the final outcome is good and that God is in control. Can you think of times in your life when your situation seemed bleak, but in the end, you could see God's hand at work? Maybe you've seen situations miraculously turn, or a failing relationship renewed, or a diagnosis reversed. From seeing God's faithfulness in the past, our hope grows that He will be ever faithful to us.

A teacher who lives with hope in her life can

also share that with her students. Often, students don't recognize their own potential, and they feel stuck academically. When a teacher can see that child's potential and offer encouragement, she can open the child's eyes to a world that had seemed off limits. Hope is one of the best gifts that a teacher can offer, because long after the child has moved on to a different class, that sense of hope will still motivate him to work hard and dream big. With renewed vision, he can strive to do something meaningful with his life.

Hope deferred makes the heart sick,
but when dreams come true,
there is life and joy.

PROVERBS 13:12 NLT

LEARNING TO DREAM

Beatrice lived with her parents in government housing and went to school in the projects. Her parents had immigrated to the States before she was born. They had both been teachers in their homeland and had enjoyed a higher station of life there. But here, they did not have much money. What they did have was education and ambition, and they passed that along to Beatrice as well.

Beatrice grew up knowing that she would go far, because her parents believed in her and had helped her to believe in herself. The teachers in her school district knew that few of their students would ever go to college, and they rarely mentioned the option. But Beatrice was an exception. She was especially bright and excelled in school. By the time she started middle school, her teachers had noticed her.

A certain math teacher thought that Beatrice would do well in a special public high school that focused on math and science at a high level. Beatrice worked very hard that year and hoped she might have a chance to get in. When she was ac-cepted into the school, Beatrice knew she was privileged to be there, so she worked very hard. Unlike most of the kids in her neighborhood, she enjoyed learning, and wanted to go to college after high school. She was also very involved with extracurricular activities and made lots of friends. Her teachers and her parents continued to encourage her as she worked through the high-level curriculum.

By the time she had to take her college entrance exam, she was nervous but decided she would attack this test as she had done all of the others. She prayed about it, gave it to God, and did her best. Her best turned out to be one of the highest scores in the nation. Suddenly her options were wide open.

Her high school counselor asked her where she wanted to go to college. Beatrice hesitated, since her parents didn't have much money. When the counselor assured her that money might not be a problem, she set her sights high. Why not Harvard? It was a shot in the dark, but Beatrice had always believed that if she worked hard, she would succeed wherever she went. She filled out pages and pages of paperwork for the application, and she wrote an essay about growing up in the projects. Even if she were accepted, it didn't mean she would be able to go. The waiting game began, and she tried to keep her mind on other things. But always in her mind were hopes of Harvard.

Two months later, she got a phone call from an admissions counselor at Harvard. She had expected a letter of acceptance or rejection, not a phone call. She anxiously held her breath, waiting for some kind of news. She grinned when the voice on the other end told her she was accepted. But she still held back, nervous about her financial situation. She paused, wondering how to ask the question, when the counselor told her that not only was she accepted, but she had also won a four-year, full-ride scholarship. Everything was paid for, including room and board.

When Beatrice hung up the phone, her mom was waiting by her side. She let out a loud whoop and started dancing around her mother, talking so fast she could hardly understand her. She had great cause to celebrate. Beatrice beat the odds. No child from their neighborhood had ever even applied to Harvard, but Beatrice had made it. Her hope had helped her achieve the impossible.

And I am sure that God,
who began the good work within you,
will continue his work until it is
finally finished on that day when
Christ Jesus comes back again.

PHILIPPIANS 1:6 NLT

CONTAGIOUS OPTIMISM

Those of us who know Christ know the one true source of hope. When we are filled with Him, we can convey that sense of hope to our students. They will be drawn to us by the encouragement and affirmation that we offer, and they will also be drawn to Christ who lives in us. Some students will ask a teacher to pray for them when they are going through tough times. The kind of hope that allows Christians to be optimistic, even during hard times, will shine brightly to the students who most need it.

But in your hearts set apart Christ as Lord. Always be prepared to give an answer to everyone who asks you to give the reason for the hope that you have. But do this with gentleness and respect, keeping a clear conscience, so that those who speak maliciously against your good behavior in Christ may be ashamed of their slander.

1 PETER 3:15–16 NIV

Song by an Old Shepherd

When silver snow decks Sylvio's clothes,
And jewel hangs at shepherd's nose,
We can abide life's pelting storm,
That makes our limbs quake, if our hearts
    be warm.

Whilst Virtue is our walking-staff,
And Truth a lantern to our path,
We can abide life's pelting storm,
That makes our limbs quake, if our hearts
    be warm.

Blow, boisterous wind, stern winter frown,
Innocence is a winter's gown.
So clad, we'll abide life's pelting storm,
That makes our limbs quake, if our hearts
    be warm.

WILLIAM BLAKE

HUMOR

*All the days of the poor are hard,
but a cheerful heart has a continual feast.*

PROVERBS 15:15 NRSV

A LIGHTHEARTED LIFE

We've often heard that laughter is the best medicine. In the classroom, laughter can be the single biggest factor for success. When a teacher is able to make the class fun and is able to recognize the funny things that she and her students say and do, she brings a sense of lighthearted joy to the room. Laughter can make even the dullest subject come alive and can draw out the most reserved students. A good dose of humor may bring a silent class to life.

If we ever get out of the habit of laughing, we need to rediscover it. We can see the world, and especially our classrooms, with the expectation that life is just funny. By keeping our eyes and ears open, we will discover the absurd and the endearing in the most unexpected places. And when students see their teachers laugh, they gain a whole new appreciation for teachers as real people.

More than anyone else, Christians have reason to laugh. The little pitfalls and setbacks in life cannot affect the security and joy of knowing Christ. As Christians, we can take ourselves less seriously by acknowledging that we are works in progress, far from complete. Jesus seemed to have a lighthearted view of the situations in His life and took every day in stride, and we can do the same. By living with that sense of joy and looking for the humor around us, we are able to live life fully, not weighed down by the seeming burdens of each day.

A joyful heart makes a cheerful face,
but when the heart is sad,
the spirit is broken.

PROVERBS 15:13 NASB

The only way to be convincingly cheerful on the outside is to have a glad heart on the inside. Growing closer to the Lord has an amazing way of lifting our hearts. Jesus set us free and came that we might have life and have it to the full. Every day is an opportunity for us to embrace that fullness.

If people please God, God will give them wisdom, knowledge, and joy. But sinners will get

only the work of gathering and storing wealth
that they will have to give to the ones who
please God. So all their work is useless, like
chasing the wind.

ECCLESIASTES 2:26 NCV

A sense of humor is like a needle and thread: It will patch up so many things.

THE VALUE OF LAUGHTER

Miss Price taught fourth grade, and she ran a tight ship. When her class walked down the hall, the students were in two perfect lines, and they marched in step. Her rules were unbendable and her face often stern. But her students knew the softer side of Miss Price.

One day Jeff came into the classroom with especially muddy shoes and tracked mud all over the room. He didn't know it until a couple of the students whispered and looked nervously at Miss Price. She shook a finger at him and sternly reprimanded, "Forty lashes with a wet noodle!" Jeff didn't quite know how to take this, since her voice sounded so stern. But her eyes had a hint of laughter in them, and it gave her away. Severe punishment indeed!

Although other students stared in awe at Miss Price, her own students knew that she wasn't the least bit mean. Her love for her students showed despite the sternness of her countenance. Because she was likely to break into an unexpected smile at any time, her students watched her closely. Because of her discipline, they obeyed her. And because she taught the class the value of a good laugh, they learned to laugh even at themselves.

When I was young, I was put in a school for retarded kids for two years before they realized I actually had a hearing loss. . .and they called me slow!

KATHY BUCKLEY

A TEACHER'S SURVIVAL KIT
FOR EVERYDAY LIVING

Toothpick–reminds us to look for the good
    qualities in our students.
You may be the only teacher who says something
    positive to them that day.

Rubber band–reminds teachers that we have
    to be flexible.
Things don't always go the way we plan,
But flexibility will help to work it out.

Band Aid–reminds teachers that sometimes we
    do more than teach,
That we help heal hurt feelings, broken dreams,
And lend an ear to a problem.

Pencil–reminds us to be thankful, and we should
    list our blessings daily,
But also encourage our students to list their
    blessings
And to be proud of their accomplishments.

Eraser–reminds us to allow students to know
    we are human
And make mistakes just like they do, and it's okay.
We must all be able to learn from our mistakes.

Chewing gum–reminds us to stick with it
And encourage our students to do likewise.
Even the impossible task or assignment can
  be accomplished
By sticking to it.

Mint–reminds us and our students we are worth
  a mint.
(We may not be paid a mint, but we are worth one.)

Candy kiss–reminds us that everyone needs a hug,
Kiss, or warm fuzzy every day.
(All teachers, students, parents, and even
  administrators)

Tea bag–reminds us we need time to relax,
Go over our blessing, and take time for others.
Family, husbands, wives, friends, children need
  quality time together.

Teachers must be willing to show their students
  how much they care!

ORIGINAL AUTHOR UNKNOWN*

---

*Adapted for teachers by Charles Nelson and his fellow teachers in
South Carolina, October 15, 1999.

WES'S LAST STAND

One year, Tasha had Wes in her seventh-grade class. Wes was an extremely vocal and overexuberant student when it came to answering questions during discussions. He always wanted to get a laugh from his friends and applause from Tasha. Wes was very smart and quite earnest in his intent to answer the question correctly. Whenever Tasha asked a question, his hand was up, often before she had finished asking the question.

This made Tasha laugh and cringe at the same time. When she called on him and he guessed the answer incorrectly, the class reacted like a game show audience. Every time he answered correctly, the class had a huge celebration. This lasted the entire year, and Tasha never knew whether she should call on him or not, since she could never control the group reaction.

On the last day of class, Tasha hosted a Civil War trivia contest in her classroom. Of course, Wes raised his hand as she began to ask the question, "Which Civil War general. . . ?" So she stopped and called on him. "All right, Wes, what's the answer?"

"Robert E. Lee," was his response. That was correct.

"That's right, Wes." Applause erupted in the room. "Now tell me," she said with a smile, knowing she could get him with her next question, "what was my question?" Tasha thought she had him there, because she was asking a fairly specific question, and Robert E. Lee certainly could be the answer to many questions about the Civil War.

"Uh. . .who was the Civil War general who was asked by Lincoln to lead the Union troops but said no?"

Tasha was dumbfounded. Wes was right. When she revealed this to the class, everyone went wild–including Tasha. They laughed for a long time. "Wes's last stand" had certainly been to Tasha's surprise, but it became one of the most memorable and humorous moments of the entire year.

REJOICE, YE PURE IN HEART

Rejoice, ye pure in heart,
Rejoice, give thanks, and sing;
Your festal banner wave on high,
The cross of Christ your King.
Rejoice, rejoice,
Rejoice, give thanks, and sing!

Still lift your standard high,
Still march in firm array;
As warriors through the darkness toil
Till dawns the golden day.
Rejoice, rejoice,
Rejoice, give thanks, and sing!

Yes, on through life's long path,
Still chanting as ye go;
From youth to age, by night and day,
In gladness and in woe.
Rejoice, rejoice,
Rejoice, give thanks, and sing!

Then on, ye pure in heart,
Rejoice, give thanks, and sing;
Your festal banner wave on high,
The cross of Christ your King.
Rejoice, rejoice,
Rejoice, give thanks, and sing!

EDWARD H. PLUMPTRE

IMAGINATION

Then God said, "Let us make human beings in our image and likeness. And let them rule over the fish in the sea and the birds in the sky, over the tame animals, over all the earth, and over all the small crawling animals on the earth."

So God created human beings in his image. In the image of God he created them. He created them male and female.

GENESIS 1:26–27 NCV

COLORFUL LEARNING

Imagine the creation of something from nothing. Perhaps we have heard these verses so many times that they have become routine to our minds. The creator's imaginative work would have been incredible to witness, as He took clay and formed a man out of it—not a sculpture, but a living, breathing man. Since we are made in His image, we too have creative abilities. The difference is that our creativity comes from Him, while He doesn't rely on anyone else in order to be creative. He created creativity itself.

As children, we were encouraged to be creative —to fingerpaint, to invent stories, to dress up, to be doctors and teachers and race car drivers, to play instruments, to color, to mold things out of clay, to sing. As children, we played creatively without the confines of self-consciousness. Our imaginations had great exercise then but sadly may have grown rusty from disuse.

When we teachers think and communicate

creatively, we appeal to our students more on their creative level. Creativity in the classroom can be as simple as jazzing up lesson plans and worksheets, or it can mean unexpected surprises or special projects for the kids. By stimulating their minds, we can keep the rhythm of the classroom fast and fun and get the kids excited about learning.

*See, I have chosen Bezalel son of Uri,
the son of Hur, of the tribe of Judah,
and I have filled him with the Spirit of God,
with skill, ability and knowledge
in all kinds of crafts—
to make artistic designs for work
in gold, silver and bronze.*

EXODUS 31:2–4 NIV

JESUS' VISUAL AIDS

Books without pictures or conversations seem very dull to children. Pictures help spark readers' imaginations and transport us to the characters' world. Lessons become far more interesting when presented as stories, even for adults. Jesus used stories to communicate His message, and His parables are very memorable. A little bit of imagination in a lesson goes a long way and doesn't have to be time-consuming to be effective.

*Imagination is
more important than knowledge.*

ALBERT EINSTEIN

ON A CREATIVE NOTE

Deborah had mild cerebral palsy, and although she functioned normally, her little body constantly made slight little jerks all the time. At first, the other third graders laughed at the way she walked, but as they got to know her, they liked her a lot and included her in games on the playground. Mrs. Harris always emphasized to her students that they needed to be friends with each other, and if they ever saw anyone playing alone, they should invite that student to join in the fun. They loved Mrs. Harris, and they wanted to please her, so they tried to remember what she told them about being nice to everyone.

While the class was learning cursive, Mrs.

Harris thought it was fun to teach them how to draw the curvy lines that connected the letters. Some of the students learned faster than others, but most of them enjoyed it. Deborah had more difficulty than most. Because of her constant jerking, her letters didn't flow smoothly together like they were supposed to, and it upset her. She wanted to be able to have neat handwriting like the other students. Mrs. Harris was aware of the frustration Deborah felt but didn't know how to help her overcome it. Deborah would simply have to learn to accept her limits, as hard as it was.

Mrs. Harris decided to create a relaxing mood while her students practiced their handwriting, so she played classical music. After she turned the music on, the students focused on their assignment, and the room became really quiet. The children seemed to concentrate more on what they were doing. As the days passed, Mrs. Harris noticed that Deborah's cursive was getting better and better. She wondered what made the difference, since most of the time Deborah's little body didn't stop making small jerks whether she was sitting down in class or walking down the hall.

One day, Mrs. Harris forgot to turn the music on. In the back of the classroom, Deborah broke her pencil and started to cry. She came up to the front and said, "Please, Mrs. Harris, put the music back on—I can't write without it!" Astonished, Mrs. Harris turned the music on, the students went back to writing, and Deborah started writing smoothly again. Mrs. Harris was amazed to discover that the rhythm of the music helped Deborah's brain to make the connection to her fingers, which then followed the command to write smoothly. Deborah became the best in the class in cursive writing. At the end of the year, when Mrs. Harris presented her with the blue ribbon for the best penmanship, little Deborah beamed with delight. Mrs. Harris learned never to ignore a creative idea, no matter how unusual it might seem.

I tried to make my classes a stimulating experience for my students. . .life experiences, creative experiences. I tried to get them to drop prejudices and conditioned responses from their thinking. In essence, I tried to teach them to embrace life openly, to reflect upon its mysteries, rejoice in its surprises, and to reject its cruelties.

PAT CONROY,
The Water Is Wide

IMPACT

Because the Teacher was wise, he taught the people everything he knew. He collected proverbs and classified them. Indeed, the Teacher taught the plain truth, and he did so in an interesting way.

A wise teacher's words spur students to action and emphasize important truths. The collected sayings of the wise are like guidance from a shepherd.

ECCLESIASTES 12:9–11 NLT

SMALL WORD, BIG IMPACT

Teachers are in a unique position to influence their students, and this is both a serious responsibility and an exciting opportunity. Teachers can make such an impact on students that their words and actions will never be forgotten. Because teachers can make both positive and negative impressions on students, the Bible clearly warns teachers of their great responsibility, which can never be taken lightly. An academic lesson may be important in the short run, but a teacher's attitude may have a more lasting effect.

When a respected teacher encourages his student to pursue a certain talent, the student may change his life direction. If a student does not receive encouragement at home, a teacher may become the most affirming influence in his life. Although teachers may never know the full impact of their words, they can be certain that they are influencing impressionable hearts.

They teach wisdom and self-control;
  they will help you understand wise words.
They will teach you how to be wise and
    self-controlled and will teach you to do what
    is honest and fair and right.
They make the uneducated smarter
    and give knowledge and sense to the young.
Wise people can also listen and learn;
    even smart people can find good advice in
      these words.
Then anyone can understand wise words and
    stories, the words of the wise and their riddles.
Knowledge begins with respect for the Lord,
    but fools hate wisdom and self-control.

PROVERBS 1:2–7 NCV

A Teacher
Takes a hand
Opens a mind
Touches a heart
Shapes the future.

AUTHOR UNKNOWN

HIDDEN TALENT, HIDDEN HOPE

In the 1930s and 1940s, Ruth Wilkinson taught art to high school students, in addition to her work as a book illustrator. During the Depression, people took any kind of work they could find, so Ruth felt blessed to have work that she actually enjoyed. The Lord had given her talent in art and also talent in teaching art, which became very satisfying for her. She taught her students how to do still lifes, sculptures, and models, and sometimes she took them outside to draw a wider landscape. She wanted to give them a broad experience with art and knew that some would be better at one skill and others better at another.

As her class progressed one year, she noticed one student who had unusual talent in drawing. Doug seemed discouraged whenever she saw him in the hall, but while he was drawing his eyes were bright, he had a little smile on his face, and he seemed relaxed and happy. He worked hard on one piece that he entered in a school contest. It came as no surprise to his art teacher when he won the competition. Ruth told him he had real potential as a professional artist, and he looked at her with wide eyes filled with hope. He didn't say a word but seized onto the compliment as if it were his lifeline.

She asked him what his parents thought about his interest in art, and Doug said that they had never noticed how much he liked it until the show. They thought it was a good hobby, but because of the Depression, they wanted him to learn a trade that would give him a good, steady income.

Ruth asked his parents to meet with her to discuss Doug's talent. At first, they were very reluctant to allow him to study art, but they were impressed that Ruth was not only an art teacher, but also a professional artist on the side. She proposed that she set up a meeting with the head of the art department at a publishing house. They agreed, and Doug feverishly put together a portfolio of his best work.

When the big day came, the head of the art department was so impressed with Doug's drawings that he not only offered to help pay for art school expenses, but he also gave him a part-time job in the meantime. Doug's unspoken dream had become a reality. He later became a well-known artist thanks to the influence of one insightful art teacher.

ETERNITY

He who binds to himself a joy
Does the winged life destroy
But he who kisses the joy as it flies
Lives in eternity's sunrise.

WILLIAM BLAKE

YOU MUST DECIDE. . .

Mrs. Randall prepared carefully for her fourth-grade science class. She had prayed at length about how to teach the difficult lesson on how the earth and people began. After presenting the theories in the science book, she concluded, "And some people believe God created everything."

A student raised his hand. "I don't believe we just happened. I think God made us."

Mrs. Randall quietly allowed the class to discuss their views. Finally one student demanded, "What do you think, Teacher?"

"I believe God made this earth and us, but you must decide for yourselves."

The class continued their dicussion and decided the same thing.

Thank You, Lord, for teaching these young minds, Mrs. Randall silently prayed.[*]

WRITTEN LEGACY

Thousands of Christians breathe, move and live, pass off the stage of life, and are heard no more—why?

They did not partake of good, and none in the world were blessed by them. None could point to them as the guide to their redemption. They wrote nothing, and nothing they said could be recalled. And so they passed on, remembered no more than insects of yesterday.

Will you live and die this way, O man immortal? Live for something. Do good, and leave behind a monument of virtue. Write your name in kindness, love, and mercy on the hearts of all you come in contact with; you will never be forgotten.

No, your name, your deeds will be as legible on the hearts you leave behind as the stars on the brow of evening. Good deeds will shine as the stars of heaven.

THOMAS CHALMERS (1780–1847)[†]

[*] Reece, Colleen L., and Anita Corrine Donihue, *Apples for a Teacher: A Bushel of Stories, Poems, and Prayers* (Uhrichsville, Ohio: Barbour Publishing, Inc., 1998), 24.
[†] "Walk with Thomas Chalmers," *Closer Walk*, May 2000 (Atlanta: Walk Thru the Bible Ministries), 14.

INSPIRATION

I will instruct you and teach you
the way you should go;
I will counsel you with my eye upon you.

PSALM 32:8 NRSV

A Captivated Mind–
What Inspires You?

Some people are inspired by a magnificent piece of music or a great work of art. Some are inspired by solitude or a walk on a beautiful day. Some find inspiration in the great words and writing of others. Still others find inspiration in their faith, in the face of a child, or in the eyes of a student who grasps a new concept.

As teachers, we must constantly tap into our source of inspiration. When we can identify what motivates us, what helps us be creative and teach at our best, we can return to that source when we need a fresh take on life or renewed energy for the classroom.

Inspired teachers inspire their students. Teachers who have a passion for their subject matter and a dedication to their students convey that in a thousand intangible ways. On the other hand, teachers who have grown bored with their material or tired of teaching also communicate that to their students.

Often, students care less about how inherently interesting a topic is than about how persuasively interesting their teacher is. An inspired teacher can transform a dull lesson on history into a captivating story about the customs of a foreign people. An inspired teacher can convey his enthusiasm about the value of a subject to his students–and they in turn will believe it is valuable, too.

After the years have passed, your students will not remember the lessons that you taught them in a certain month of a particular year, but they will remember you and the feelings of inspiration you passed on to them.

CREATIVE APPLAUSE

Mark liked innovation. He thought creativity helped students learn and forced teachers to continually improve their styles, too. Mark often sought change just for the sake of doing something new. He accepted a new job at a new school so that he could learn a new method of teaching.

But Mark's new environment did not encourage innovation. Suddenly, he found himself in a rigid system with highly competent but very reserved teachers. The teachers acted very independently and rarely shared ideas, suggestions, or problems. Mark felt stifled, but he determined not to give up trying.

While Mark was teaching an especially difficult math lesson, he noticed that the students were having a hard time understanding it. Their eyes had started to wander, and they shared the same frustrated expression that he assumed must be on his face. Mark knew it was time for a change.

Without any warning, he started clapping. The kids looked instantly up at him. He clapped out a few rhythms to help them memorize the math facts. With big smiles on their faces, they started clapping along with him. When a student got confused on the clapping, Mark reviewed it again, and then they all tried it together. They loved it, and they learned the math facts to help them with the harder concepts.

One of the teachers on Mark's team was very rigid in her lessons. She was a gifted mathematician who could have taught at the college level, and she was very structured in the way she taught the different concepts. After they had been working together for a few months, Nancy felt inspired by Mark's creativity. One day Mark noticed that Nancy had all of her students down on the floor with newspapers, experimenting with a different way of understanding math.

Mark's streak of inspiration had left its mark. His students never forgot that math lesson, Nancy developed a new teaching style, and Mark found the freedom to experiment once again.

*But it is the spirit in a person,
the breath of the Almighty,
that gives understanding.*

JOB 32:8 NCV

TEAMWORK

Homeschooling your children can be an overwhelming task. When Andrea first started teaching at home, she looked over tons of curriculum and tried to pick the best combinations. She worked on lessons, researched teaching methods, and read thoroughly over her materials.

But she did much more than that. Knowing that she would need extra creativity and support, Andrea joined a network of other homeschool parents and kids. Not only did she look forward to their meetings and activities, but she also relied heavily on them for inspiration in the classroom.

The teachers in the network shared ideas about anything and everything in the classroom, from project ideas to teaching tips to book recommendations. Whenever Andrea had a question about teaching, she asked the group for input. Other teachers brought such different perspectives to the group that they all benefited from the collective experience. Andrea learned new ideas that she never would have developed on her own.

THE SOUND OF THE SEA

The sea awoke at midnight from its sleep,
And round the pebbly beaches far and wide
I heard the first wave of the rising tide
Rush onward with uninterrupted sweep;
A voice out of the silence of the deep,
A sound mysteriously multiplied
As of a cataract from the mountain's side,
Or roar of winds upon a wooded steep.
So comes to us at times, from the unknown
And inaccessible solitudes of being,
The rushing of the sea-tides of the soul;
And inspirations, that we deem our own,
Are some divine foreshadowing and foreseeing
Of things beyond our reason or control.
Sit in reverie and watch the changing color of
    the waves that break
upon the idle seashore of the mind.

HENRY WADSWORTH LONGFELLOW

JOY

The unfailing love of the LORD never ends!
By his mercies we have been kept
from complete destruction.
Great is his faithfulness;
his mercies begin afresh each day.
I say to myself, "The LORD is my inheritance;
therefore, I will hope in him!"

LAMENTATIONS 3:22–24 NLT

ETERNAL JOY

True joy is rooted in Christ. Apart from Him, it is possible to experience fleeting happiness or moments of joy, but only those who know Jesus can really have that deep, unshakable joy that is independent of life circumstances. Only those who have placed their lives in His care can truly let go of their burdens and live freely with joy.

Happiness is a good feeling that is tied to how good life seems at any given moment. But joy is much deeper than happiness, and Jesus enables us to live with a sense of joy even when situations or relationships in our lives are less than perfect. Joy is possible because He is the end of all things, and the final outcomes of our lives and eternity have ultimately been determined. If we can live with that truth stamped on our minds, we can embrace the joy that Jesus offers to those who follow Him with all their hearts.

For the joy of the LORD is your strength.

NEHEMIAH 8:10 NIV

A JOYFUL RHYTHM

Gary felt burned out. He had always loved teaching, but now he felt like he just went through the motions. The rest of his life seemed fine. He enjoyed playing with his boys in the park, and his marriage had never been better. His relationship with the Lord was dynamic and growing, and he stayed very involved at church. But the spark, the joy, had gone out of his work. His reviews showed that he was still a good teacher, but it wasn't enough.

An old friend from college called Gary one weekend and invited him to visit a class for inner-city kids. It was a dynamic new way of teaching at-risk students that helped them enjoy learning. It sounded interesting, so Gary accepted the invitation. But when he walked into his friend's classroom, he was not prepared for what he saw.

The kids were in their music class, and the teacher was letting the students help him write a musical that they would be performing. He was actually composing during the class by giving the students different options to choose from. These kids were a lively bunch, at times unruly, but the teacher did not allow misbehavior. The atmosphere felt fun and upbeat. As Gary listened to the words of the song, he realized that this was much more than a music class—it was a math class. They were learning about math through music, and the kids were totally into the rhythm—clapping hands, tapping shoes, and drumming the backs of the chairs in front of them. The teacher encouraged their participation but curtailed anything that sounded like whining or fighting.

Several times throughout the class period, the teacher asked them a question that they answered as a class, reciting together, "We are very, very smart!"

Gary was impressed. The style of teaching was totally unique—physical movement, rhythm, positive reinforcement, creativity. Without a doubt, if these students were able to continue in this type of program, they would not only stay off the streets and out of gangs more, but many of the students would go far. After the class ended, Gary found out more about the program. Apparently, they had generous donors so they could hire top-notch professionals to teach the kids for free.

As he drove home that night, Gary had a

renewed appreciation for his work as a teacher. With open eyes, he realized the privilege he had to teach kids who didn't face as many obstacles. Although any job could become monotonous, Gary felt a new excitement for his work. Nothing about his job had changed, but his perspective had changed.

Shout for joy to the LORD, all the earth.
Worship the LORD with gladness;
come before him with joyful songs.
Know that the LORD is God.
It is he who made us, and we are his;
we are his people, the sheep of his pasture.

Enter his gates with thanksgiving
and his courts with praise;
give thanks to him and praise his name.
For the LORD is good and his love endures forever;
his faithfulness continues through all
generations.

PSALM 100 NIV

PEACE

If I go up to the heavens, you are there;
    if I make my bed in the depths, you are there.
If I rise on the wings of the dawn,
    if I settle on the far side of the sea,
even there your hand will guide me,
    your right hand will hold me fast.

PSALM 139:8–10 NIV

The Source of Peace

Peaceful" might be the last word you would choose to describe your classroom at times. Perhaps your room seems more like chaos or widespread panic than peace, and the only moments of quiet come when the more active students seem to drowse off. Or perhaps you achieve peace in the classroom at the cost of something else, like participation or creativity or your own sanity. Whatever your situation might be, you undoubtedly have moments of both joy and stress in the classroom.

As a teacher, you must be able to respond to a hundred different questions, problems, concerns, and unexpected moments each day. In order to live up to the demands on your time, you need a reserve to draw from, a source of strength to fall back on. During those times, nothing can replace a deep sense of peace.

Christ has made unquenchable peace available to those who believe. Regardless of what is going on around you–activity, chaos, learning, talking, noise—you can rest in the peace that passes under-standing. Even if you feel overwhelmed or inade-quate, God will make you equal to your tasks. And the peace of Christ will rule in your heart as you trust Him to carry all of your concerns.

> *God is our refuge and strength,*
> *an ever-present help in trouble.*
> *Therefore we will not fear, though the earth*
> *give way*
> *and the mountains fall into the heart of*
> *the sea,*
> *though its waters roar and foam*
> *and the mountains quake with their*
> *surging.*
> *There is a river whose streams make glad the*
> *city of God,*
> *the holy place where the Most High dwells.*
> PSALM 46:1–4 NIV

PERSISTENT PRAYER

For as long as Jeremy Patton has taught sixth grade, he has followed a daily routine of arriving in his classroom at 6:00 A.M. to pray over every desk and for every student in his class. He trusts

God to fill him with the peace for each new day.

One year Jeremy had a boy in his class who had severe emotional problems. He had a brilliant mind and seemed to come from a good home, but his anger and violence were uncontrollable. At times, Robert threw tables in anger. With his bright mind, he also constantly challenged Jeremy.

Every morning, Jeremy faithfully prayed for Robert. He did not see changes overnight, but he did see changes. Robert started asking fewer belligerent questions and started to show signs of respect. About halfway through the year, Robert began to smile occasionally, and Jeremy knew that God was planting seeds of peace in his life. Eventually, he smiled frequently and began to talk more to other kids.

One day Jeremy had a particularly difficult concept to teach. The students weren't getting it. Just as Jeremy's frustration piqued, Robert stood up, walked to the front of the class, and politely asked Jeremy if he could try. His brilliant young mind had grasped the concept, and he had the ability to speak to the class on their level so they would understand it.

After that day, the other students began to like Robert more, and he began to fit in with the other boys better. Jeremy was amazed. His most difficult, violent, angry student had changed so much, and he knew that the Lord had brought peace where there had only been anger. His prayers had been answered.

As for me, far be it from me that I should sin against the LORD by failing to pray for you. And I will teach you the way that is good and right.

1 SAMUEL 12:23 NIV

A ROWDY CLASSROOM

Daniel came home from school every day with upsetting stories. It seemed as if his teacher, Mr. McClure, simply could not control his classroom. Daniel said the class was out of control, and he wasn't learning anything. Marion's heart sank at her son's words.

They lived in a weak school district, Marion knew, and the classes were crowded. She called the principal and discovered that Mr. McClure was a first-year teacher. They were strapped for good teachers, the principal told her, and they had to use everyone they had. The other teachers had their own hands too full to help him. He would have to learn how to gain control of the class and how to be the authority figure. If the principal and other teachers kept stepping in, the students would never respect him.

Marion hung up somewhat discouraged and wondered what she could do. Moving to a better district was not an option. At least she could pray.

Marion prayed faithfully for Mr. McClure several times each day. She asked the Lord to give him wisdom, respect, and authority in his classroom. She continued praying for the rest of the school year, and Daniel began bringing home news about the good changes. When Marion found out that several other parents were also Christians, she encouraged them to pray for Mr. McClure, too.

By the end of the year, Mr. McClure had much better control of the class, and the students were actually learning. Marion had learned a valuable lesson, and she continued to pray for Daniel's teachers every year.

And let the peace of Christ rule in your hearts, to which indeed you were called in the one body. And be thankful. Let the word of Christ dwell in you richly; teach and admonish one another

in all wisdom; and with gratitude in your
hearts sing psalms, hymns, and spiritual songs
to God. And whatever you do, in word or deed,
do everything in the name of the Lord Jesus, giv-
ing thanks to God the Father through him.

COLOSSIANS 3:15–17 NRSV

FIRST DAY THOUGHTS

In calm and cool and silence, once again
I find my old accustomed place among
My brethren, where, perchance, no human
    tongue
Shall utter words; where never hymn is sung,
Nor deep-toned organ blown, nor censer
    swung,
Nor dim light falling through the pictured
    pane!
There, syllabled by silence, let me hear
The still small voice which reached the
    prophet's ear;
Read in my heart a still diviner law
Than Israel's leader on his tables saw!
There let me strive with each besetting sin,
Recall my wandering fancies, and restrain
The sore disquiet of a restless brain;

And, as the path of duty is made plain,
May grace be given that I may walk therein,
Not like the hireling, for this selfish gain,
With backward glances and reluctant tread,
Making a merit of his coward dread,
But, cheerful, in the light around me thrown,
Walking as one to pleasant service led;
Doing God's will as if it were my own,
Yet trusting not in mine, but in His strength
    alone!

JOHN GREENLEAF WHITTIER

REFRESHMENT

*I will refresh the weary
and satisfy the faint.*

JEREMIAH 31:25 NIV

THIRSTY FOR CHRIST

At times, teaching can drain our strength. Not only do we invest hours of time and preparation into our work, but we also invest much of ourselves into our students. Sometimes we pour ourselves out completely, and we feel the need for refreshment. As rewarding as teaching can be, we cannot continue to give and give without being replenished. For times such as this, we may need to set aside time for rest and ask the Lord to refresh us.

We can find rest even in the midst of a busy schedule. It may be as simple as a change in pace or a new activity that will bring a fresh perspective to the routine. Or we may look for some time away, extra sleep, or more exercise. Most importantly, we can offer our burdens and frustrations to God and ask Him to restore us to full strength. By spending time in prayer with Him, we can draw on His infinite resources of strength and patience. These can become special times of refreshment for our spirits, like the morning dew that covers the grass.

The LORD upholds all those who fall
  and lifts up all who are bowed down.
The eyes of all look to you,
  and you give them their food at the proper time.
You open your hand
  and satisfy the desires of every living thing.

PSALM 145:14–16 NIV

The true way to live is to
enjoy every moment as it passes,
and surely it is in the everyday things
around us that the beauty of life lies.

LAURA INGALLS WILDER

GETTING RECHARGED

Sarah knew she needed a break. She had been dragging through life for several weeks, and she needed a change of scenery. She set aside Saturday for some time alone.

When Saturday arrived, Sarah overlooked her "To Do" list and set out for her day. Without rest, she knew that she could never face another week, so she drove two hours south to a state park. She had never been there before, and the prospect of an adventure excited her.

The day started off with light rain, but by the time Sarah arrived at the park, the skies had cleared. She saw no other people on the trail, so she began hiking in silence, alone with her thoughts. She felt so far from the congestion of the city, and she saw her setting with new eyes. As she walked, she prayed quietly and felt herself drawn closer to God's presence. *What a relief not to be correcting homework or getting ready for the next day,* she thought.

Sarah began to notice more of her surroundings. Bright sun broke out across the meadow in front of her. A few early spring flowers poked through the grass. She couldn't remember the last time she felt so relaxed or had so much fun. A few people showed up on the trails later in the afternoon, and there was a camaraderie among them that never occurred in the city between strangers.

At the end of the day, Sarah drove home, watching the few clouds in the sky turn every shade of peach and mauve and finally deep purple as the sun disappeared. She felt as if she had been away for a week. With renewed energy, she prepared for a fresh start on her life.

Come to me, all you that are weary and are carrying heavy burdens, and I will give you rest. Take my yoke upon you, and learn from me; for I am gentle and humble in heart, and you will find rest for your souls. For my yoke is easy, and my burden is light.

MATTHEW 11:28–30 NRSV

WHEN I CONSIDER
HOW MY LIGHT IS SPENT

When I consider how my light is spent,
Ere half my days, in this dark world and wide,
And that one talent which is death to hide,
Lodged with me useless,
    though my soul more bent
To serve therewith my Maker, and present
My true account, lest He returning chide;
"Doth God exact day-labor, light denied?"
I fondly ask; but Patience to prevent
That murmur, soon replies, "God doth not need
Either man's work or His own gifts; who best
Bear His mild yoke, they serve Him best. His state
Is kingly. Thousands at His bidding speed
And post o'er land and ocean without rest:
They also serve who only stand and wait."

JOHN MILTON

SATISFACTION

Not that I was ever in need, for I have learned how to get along happily whether I have much or little. I know how to live on almost nothing or with everything. I have learned the secret of living in every situation, whether it is with a full stomach or empty, with plenty or little. For I can do everything with the help of Christ who gives me the strength I need.

PHILIPPIANS 4:11–13 NLT

A Choice and a Blessing

Paul speaks with authority about being content, regardless of his life circumstances. Because he placed his hope fully in Christ, no external event could shake his well-being. Paul made a choice to be content, and we can do the same.

Satisfaction is a powerful feeling that involves contentment about life without pride for our own accomplishments. Satisfaction is a gift from God. We can choose to be satisfied, and we can ask the Lord to provide that sense of contentment that only He can give.

Those who are able to take satisfaction in their work are truly blessed. Teaching offers a form of satisfaction that few people enjoy–the satifaction of shaping impressionable minds. Teachers delight in the expression of comprehension that crosses a student's face. Teachers witness firsthand the transformation that knowledge and personal attention can bring in their students.

Then I realized that it is good and proper for a man to eat and drink, and to find satisfaction in his toilsome labor under the sun during the few days of life God has given him—for this is his lot. Moreover, when God gives any man wealth and possessions, and enables him to enjoy them, to accept his lot and be happy in his work—this is a gift of God.

ECCLESIASTES 5:18–19 NIV

Father, today it all felt so right.
The children were joyously absorbed
in what they were learning,
and I moved among them full of
the satisfaction of a job well done.

ELSBETH CAMPBELL MURPHY,
Chalkdust: Prayer Meditations for Teachers

A JOB WELL DONE

Even though Janet was only in the sixth grade, she carried herself in a very sensual manner. Who knows where she learned it? Little Janet also had a very low opinion of herself. The first day of class, when she introduced herself to her teacher, Mrs. Kimball, Janet said, "Please don't expect good grades from me, because I'm really stupid." Mrs. Kimball assured her that she didn't believe it.

Throughout the year, Mrs. Kimball looked for ways to affirm Janet. On Janet's first writing assignment, Mrs. Kimball commended her on how good her penmanship was and the way she formed her characters. Even though Janet's grammar was terrible, Mrs. Kimball did not emphasize that. On every student's paper, she commented on the positive aspects. The papers showed areas where each student could improve.

As Mrs. Kimball affirmed Janet over and over, as she improved in her schoolwork, and as she heard again and again how smart she was and how much she was improving, Janet tried harder. She began to develop in other areas, as well. Janet was very athletic, so she joined the track team. This too boosted her confidence. Her self image began to improve, and she began to blossom. She had started the year as a tough kid with a sensual attitude, but as she improved in school and excelled in track, her outer defenses came down.

Mrs. Kimball watched the process with pleasure. Over time, the change in Janet was so obvious, and Mrs. Kimball knew that she had played a key part in the girl's transformation. With satisfaction, she realized how rewarding her career had become.

SATISFACTION VERSUS STATUS

Bryce had taught science for many years, and he loved his job. He liked his material, his students, and the process of teaching. Students responded well to Bryce, partly because they could tell just how much he liked them.

One year the position of principal opened, and he was encouraged to apply. The school board members had known Bryce for many years and were impressed with his ability. They unanimously voted to hire him, and he accepted. Thus began the worst year of Bryce's career.

Instead of grading papers, he shuffled through administrative paperwork. Instead of talking with students after class, he only talked with them when discipline problems arose. Instead of teaching science lessons, he managed the same teachers who had been his colleagues. Every night, he went home exhausted from the stress and strain that had become a regular part of his day. He looked forward to weekends now and dreaded Monday mornings.

The larger paycheck just did not compensate for a job that didn't offer personal satisfaction. At the end of the year, Bryce demoted himself back to his teaching position. He felt so relieved to slip back into the familiar setting of his classroom. There, he found great satisfaction and motivation, and he was never tempted to move on again.

Patient Grissill

Art thou poor, yet hast thou golden
    slumbers?
O sweet content!
Art thou rich, yet is thy mind perplexed?
O punishment!
Dost thou laugh to see how fools are vexed
To add to golden numbers, golden numbers?
O sweet content! O sweet, O sweet content!
Work apace, apace, apace, apace;
Honest labour bears a lovely face;
Then hey nonny nonny, hey nonny nonny!

Canst drink the waters of the crisped spring?
O sweet content!
Swimm'st thou in wealth, yet sink'st in
    thine own tears?
O punishment!
Then he that patiently want's burden bears
No burden bears, but is a king, a king:
O sweet content! O sweet, O sweet content!
Work apace, apace, apace, apace;
Honest labour bears a lovely face;
Then hey nonny nonny, hey nonny nonny!

Thomas Dekker

TEAMWORK

If you have any encouragement from being united with Christ, if any comfort from his love, if any fellowship with the Spirit, if any tenderness and compassion, then make my joy complete by being like-minded, having the same love, being one in spirit and purpose. Do nothing out of selfish ambition or vain conceit, but in humility consider others better than yourselves. Each of you should look not only to your own interests, but also to the interests of others. Your attitude should be the same as that of Christ Jesus.

PHILIPPIANS 2:1–5 NIV

THE STRENGTH OF MANY

Teamwork exponentially increases the potential of individuals. By relying on others who have complementary gifts and experiences, we can build on our collective strengths. By sharing burdens with those around us, we can ensure that we don't have to shoulder the load alone. When we can assign work based on the strengths and interests of the individuals on a team, we can concentrate on our own parts and do those to the best of our abilities.

As the teaching profession relies more and more on team efforts, we must learn to work well on teams. Cohesive teams can make learning a smoother process and can help students connect the concepts they learn in one class with what they are learning in their other subjects. Some teams may come together naturally, without any conflicts or barriers. Others may have to work to make the team successful. By developing an open atmosphere of support and unity, we can make other teachers feel more comfortable and help our students maximize their learning.

> *Work hard and cheerfully*
> *at whatever you do,*
> *as though you were working for the Lord*
> *rather than for people.*

COLOSSIANS 3:23 NLT

AFTER THE FINAL BELL

Emily Della Torre tried to treat everyone at her school with respect, regardless of their positions. She kept in mind that the custodians of the school often are overlooked, so she tried to see things from their perspective. When they came into a messy classroom at the end of the day, they must have felt discouraged. All their hard work to keep the school clean was undone every day, and they had to begin again. They saw papers and pencils on the floor, dirty marker boards, and disheveled desks.

Emily left her room particularly messy one day after she and her students worked on a big art project together. She wrote a quick note to the custodian, apologized for the mess, and thanked him for cleaning it up.

Later that year, she and her students made an oversized card to the community, which they hung on the outside of the school so that everyone walking or driving by could read it. Emily couldn't help but notice that whenever the wind tore a side of it off the wall, the custodian appeared quickly to fasten it back. He personally ensured that the outdoor art project stayed in good shape.

Emily realized then what a limited role she played at the school. Without the work of so many others who supported her behind the scenes, she could never accomplish as much with her students as she was able to do. She gained a new appreciation for the meaning of teamwork in her school.

TEACHERS: TEAM PLAYERS

Gloria has experienced the best and the worst of team teaching. During her first year as a teacher, Gloria found herself on a team crippled by interpersonal problems. Two of the five teachers worked closely together and excluded the other three. They communicated only between themselves. They created lesson plans together, even though the other teachers also taught some of the same subjects. Gloria felt excluded and overlooked, and her team experience made her first year even more difficult.

But Gloria has also experienced the other extreme, and she has been convinced of the power of constructive teamwork. Gloria's second team came together quickly, and they learned to balance each other. Over time, they began to enjoy each other's company so much that they also spent time together outside of school. They created a supportive environment for growth.

Jill, the team leader, had natural leadership gifts. She shared her vision, delegated the tasks, and spoke for the team in school meetings. Janet played a very different role by looking for ways to liven up the team meetings. She coordinated team social events and planned fun dinners for the group. She continually looked for ways to serve. Natalia was the quiet, reserved voice of sensibility on the team. When others began to exaggerate, she grounded them with reason. Her listening abilities and emotional support held the team together. Julie gave the team a fresh look at life with her smiles and encouraging words. She helped the team relax. Gloria was the organizer of the team, or the taskmaster. When Jill delegated, Gloria translated those goals into